UPSKILL

YOUR LEADERSHIP

LEADERSHIP LESSONS FROM LEADERSHIP SPECIALIST
ANTON GUINEA

First published by The Rural Publishing Company.

Copyright © Anton Guinea 2023.

eBook: 978-0-6458801-4-4
Print: 978-0-6458801-1-3

The Rural Publishing Company
Email: hello@theruralpublishingcompany.com.au
Website: https://theruralpublishingcompany.com.au

THIS IS THE MOST IMPORTANT BOOK DEDICATION YOU WILL READ.

This book is dedicated to all of those leaders out there who have never received leadership training. Particularly the few that come through our training programs and say that they didn't know leadership training was a thing...I nearly cried. I couldn't believe that this person, a leader for thirty years, didn't know they could come and spend two days with me and our team, and upskill themselves on how to more effectively lead others.

This book is dedicated to those leaders out there who think they've got it covered. 'I know leadership' you'll hear them say. Or 'what can you teach me about leading others?' they might think. Or even 'you can't learn leadership in a classroom.' It's a sad fact that I have heard all of these from leaders who think that the way they were taught or shown is still the right way to lead, and their old style will work in this day and age. Let's all take a deep breath for them, and wish them, and their teams, well. Our hearts go out to you all.

It's those teams, and team members, who this book is also dedicated to. Those team members that feel sick (yes, this happens) when they have to deal with their leader. Those team members who don't feel heard. Those team members who don't feel valued. Those team members that don't feel safe in their workplace.

I was one of those workers, in one of those teams. I suffered through poor leadership, and I'm committed to helping the old-school leaders who are willing to learn to upskill themselves on how to be better at leading others.

Upskilling yourself on leadership is about just that. Learning new skills. Learning how you can improve. Learning what works for others. Learning about different approaches that you can adopt, in different situations, to get different outcomes, and build better relationships. Upskilling yourself on leadership is about leaning into learning about leadership, so that you can continue to evolve and continue to become that leader that your team and organisation needs and deserves.

If you read the paragraphs above, and you're a little freaked out, don't be. You have two options: you can put this book down and never look at it again, or you can work through it, and see what happens to your mindset, and to your approach to leadership. And see what happens to your team and your team members after you apply what you've learnt.

This book is also dedicated to all of the amazing mentors, coaches and trainers, who I have learnt so much from over the years. I've invested hundreds of thousands of dollars into my professional education, not only to be the leader that my team and business needs, but so I can share what I've learnt with you—the leader who's ready to upskill their leadership!

Finally, this book is also dedicated to my amazing family, Mrs G (the amazing teacher), Toby (Son 1—engineer), and Zac (Son 2—future pilot) who've been on this crazy journey with me since 2004. They are my tribe, my number 1 team, and they are my motivation to be the best human and leader that I can be.

HOW TO USE THIS BOOK

This book is a playbook, not a story book.

It comprises a series of standalone ideas, elements, and tips and tricks to help you. It comes with actions to take to become a better thinker, a better leader, and a better advocate for your team's professional development. You'll also find a series of prompts and questions to encourage you to reflect honestly on your leadership skills and practices, and to think of ways to upgrade, upskill, and uplift yourself and your team.

Happy reading! You're on the way to being the best leader that YOU can be.

UPSKILL
YOUR LEADERSHIP

WITH THE UPSKILL MODEL

This model was developed as a strategic tool for putting theory into practice to upskill your leadership.

The model draws on various psychological theories relating to attitude, perception, and emotional experience in the workplace, and structures this information into a practical framework to guide leaders through the process of upskilling their leadership to become better leaders.

It was developed over nearly 20 years of theoretical analysis combined with real-world experience, and it underpins the Guinea Group's winning formula for creating effective leaders, high-performing teams, and workplaces that are both physically and psychologically safe for workers.

Refer back to this model while reading this book. It'll help you form a concrete framework in your mind that will, over time, become a natural reference point as you grow and develop in your attitudes and behaviours, and move you closer to being the leader you want to be.

To make the most of this resource, contact us via our website at antonguinea.com.au for a self-diagnostic tool and action plan to review and improve your skills against the model.

01
CREATE **CONSCIOUS CONTROL**
Skillset: Learn to respond, not react, to BOOM events

02
HAVE HIGH **CARE FACTOR**
Skillset: Learn how to be a good human, and a good leader

03
DEVELOP **YOUR EQ**
Skillset: Lead with emotional intelligence, and social intelligence

04
LEAD **UNDER PRESSURE**
Skillset: Stay in control and lead well even when the pressure rises

05
BE **COURAGEOUS**
Skillset: Take action when it matters, even if it scares you

CONTENTS

INTRODUCTION:
UPSKILL YOUR LEADERSHIP

Leadership can be challenging. It can be rewarding. After parenting, it's the most important job on planet Earth (sorry first responders and teachers). And it takes a range of skills and experiences to get it right.

But sitting above the skill sets of leaders are a set of three mandates. The definition of a mandate is an order or being commissioned to do something. The three leadership mandates are the obligations of leaders, from the day that they take on a leadership role. And the mandates are prioritised in this order: a mandate to the organisation, a mandate to the team, and a mandate to the self. Also known as values, transformation, and control (VTC).

Here's how to apply the BIG 3 Leadership Mandates.

ONE VALUES ALIGNMENT.

Here's the background to this mandate, the values-based and organisational-focused mandate.

When leaders (particularly senior leaders) leave organisations, especially when they've had a long tenure with that organisation, the comment that they most often make in my coaching is that: 'My values don't align with the values of the business.'

This is code for: the business has asked me to do something, to say something, to decide something that doesn't feel right, on a very deep level.

Let's slow it down a little at this point. I get that leaders sometimes must support organisational decisions and make those decisions their own. Understood. But there are times when, for the leader, this requirement violates a deep personal value.

So, the mandate for a leader is to be firstly very clear on their own set of three values. The most common leadership value is integrity. Yours might be different. Mine personally are energy, engagement, and enterprise thinking. I have a purpose that sits above those values (my 'why') which is to leave humans and businesses better than I found them.

Yours might be respect, teamwork, or any of the multitude of other values that could drive your behaviour. And that's why values are the very first mandate. Research finds that individual values are a driving force behind personal responsibility[16] (Mirvis & Googins, 2010). Again, your values drive your behaviour. They're the first things that you turn to when it comes to making big decisions.

And here's the thing: 90% of leaders (that we train and deal with at least) have never done a values exercise. They've never done the work to understand what their personal values are.

Just Google a values list, and see what words come up, and what resonates for you. Then compare your list to the values of your organisation.

And then, most importantly, understand if your values align with the organisation's values. If they don't, that's cool, you may be able to find a way to reconcile that within yourself. But if you can't, it'll be difficult to stay in your organisation for the long haul.

An understanding and alignment of values is a big thing for leaders. That's why it's mandate number one. When you're being values-driven, you can then step into transformational leadership.

TWO TRANSFORMATIONAL LEADERSHIP.

Here's the background to this mandate, the team- and human-focused mandate for leaders.

In 1978, James Burns[6] published the seminal work on transformational leadership in the book simply titled Leadership. According to Burns, transforming leadership is a process in which leaders and followers help each other to advance to a higher level of morale and motivation.

In short, here's a very quick way to sum up the concept of being a transformational leader: create more leaders. A leader's role is to work with those in their team, to provide them with the coaching, the mentoring, the training and any other opportunity for growth they need to become even better future leaders. Leaders who also understand these three mandates.

And, yes, I hear you, again. Not all our team members want to advance their careers into more senior roles. And some think that they should be progressing faster than they really should. With every mandate comes a quandary. And this is the quandary for leaders: who, and how, to develop more leaders.

There's one way to find out, and that's to have career conversations. Not performance discussions, not mid-year reviews, but career conversations. Conversations that talk through what the team member values (see mandate one), and what they want to do with their working life. For more information on this one, see the book Radical Candor by Kim Scott.[24] Some of your team might want to own a hobby farm in the future. And wouldn't it be good if you could equip them with the leadership skills to make that happen? While they're in your team, and while they're growing and producing more for your business, now.

In your team, you have rock stars and super stars (Credit: Kim Scott).[24] Rock stars want to be high performers now, and don't want to progress (so let's not force them to). Super stars want to progress (so let's understand what this progression looks like). And that progression might be quicker than you think it should be, as their leader. Some super stars are just committed to their career growth (but please presume positive intent here—it'll be for the right reasons).

I get the career focus. As a young leader, there was no way I was going to slow down and back off on my goals. I had them in a project Gannt Chart and was totally committed to progressing through the ranks. And I had leaders who supported that. Finally, I got promoted to middle-level management (too young, and too early), and I was working for a human without conscious control and with zero personal control. And that's why I do what I do now, so that leaders are better equipped than that leader was to stay in conscious control.

THREE CREATED CONSCIOUS CONTROL.

Here's the background to this mandate, the self- (and situation-) focused mandate for leaders.

It's long been known—even before we could study the human brain with high-powered technology—that the human has two thinking and behavioural pathways. One could be called the primitive, or the instinctive, or the emotional pathway. The other would be called the thinking, the reasoning, or the rational pathway.

In other words, we have instinctive and reasoning pathways for making decisions, and they both drive our behaviour. The instinctive pathway is routed through the amygdala, in the limbic system, which controls our emotional responses and our fight-or-flight response. The reasoning pathway is routed through our frontal lobes, the parts of our brain which make us uniquely human, and which allow us to plan and make rational decisions, even if the rest of our brain is trying to lose it.

Daniel Kahneman[12] called these system one and two processes, in his book Thinking Fast and Slow. In 1924, Fredrick Mathias Alexander[i] published what was at the time a very progressive book, Constructed Conscious Control of the Individual. My favourite quote from that book is:

> I do not know of any person who doubts that if people are to evolve in the right direction, the gap between the instinctive and conscious control of the self must be bridged.

Stop for a moment and reread that quote. That was written in 1924. In other words, the human must have control of self. And yes, it's still as relevant now as it was nearly one hundred years ago. Here at TGG, we call it 'created conscious control.' And conscious leadership (a more contemporary term).

Created conscious control is about emotional control, behavioural control, and situational control. And for every leader on planet Earth, this is a key mandate. To remain in control, regardless of what's happening.

Is that possible? Of course not.

But is it an obligation of leadership? Absolutely.

There are only three things that drive our behaviour, and they are our beliefs (subconsciously), our values (consciously—see mandate one), and our emotional state. And if you don't think our emotions drive our behaviour, just watch an angry person. See what damage people do to other humans, and to their own reputation, when they act on emotion rather than on reasoning.

This mandate is the self-mandate because it's incumbent upon leaders to have conscious control. Without conscious control, leaders don't have behavioural control, and without behavioural control, leaders have zero chance of having situational control. And with leaders being under so much pressure, they need to be able to manage high-pressure situations and high-stress encounters. That's the job at times.

When leaders let their emotions drive their behaviours, and when those emotions are out of control, they hurt other humans. And if they're not on the The Dark Triad,[17] they will apologise for their behaviour, and make the excuse that it was just because of their emotional state (uncool).

This is what some leaders don't understand. The hurt that leaders cause humans will be remembered for decades. How do I know? Because I ask people in our coaching and training programs for the leader conversation or conversations that hurt their hearts. Some can remember those conversations from ten, twenty, or even thirty years ago.

Knowing this, why not be the leader who's remembered for being in conscious control, and not as the leader who didn't have that control?

Creating conscious control can be learnt—it's a skill. It's a set of behaviours, habits, and patterns that a leader runs to keep their frontal lobes oxygenated and in charge of the situation. See Daniel Goleman's[11] work on Emotional Intelligence for more information on staying in emotional control.

So, there you have it. The BIG THREE leadership mandates, and why they're important.

Yes, these are simple to say. Not as easy to implement. But worth it, if you're serious about upskilling your leadership.

SKILL I

CREATE CONSCIOUS CONTROL

IF I WAS TO ASK YOU WHAT'S THE MOST IMPORTANT CHARACTER TRAIT IN YOUR LEADER, WHAT WOULD YOUR ANSWER BE?

And more importantly, if I was to ask your team what they think are the most important character traits in a leader, what would they say?

Well, at the end of last year, we asked. We reached out to my LinkedIn tribe to find out what they thought it was, and we gave people the options of clarity, consistency, charisma, and care factor.

Of the 52 respondents, the results were:

- Clarity – 14%
- Consistency – 40%
- Charisma – 2%
- Care factor – 44%

Yes, there were only a few options provided. Granted, it's only 52 responses. Also yes, consistency and care factor rated the highest. Forget charisma (a trait associated with psychopathy—as we know from the negative leadership styles in Paulhus & Williams'[18] The Dark Triad).

When I reached out and asked some of the respondents (that I knew), they were able to talk through what consistency meant for them. Put simply, it was 'consistency of emotional state'. The care factor was self-explanatory. We all know that team members don't care how much you know until they know how much you care.

So, what does this little survey tell us? That leaders who are consistent in their emotional states will connect more with their teams. And emotional control is easy when things are good. But when everything goes BOOM— well, that's a different story.

Leaders need to stay in control. By creating conscious control.

BECAUSE RESPONDING IS MORE IMPORTANT THAN REACTING

My old boss would go red, his veins would pop out of his head, and he would literally explode with rage. And venom. And aggression. Don't be like my old boss. It's not a cool look. And it hurts people!

I think the challenge for him, looking back on it, was that he just didn't have the ability to take half a second and reflect before reacting. It wasn't responding. It was all reaction.

Emotional control is a learnt skill. It really is. We have this primitive brain that reacts to stimulus in a fraction of a second, and our emotions go crazy. Unless we can turn our smart brain on and make it override that reaction, with self-talk, and by being rational, not irrational. And then respond to the stimulus, in a more controlled way.

Deepak Chopra[9] stated it best in his book The Soul of Leadership where he wrote that:

> **Emotions are closely tied to belief, ego, and past conditioning. When you get angry at someone, you're also saying 'I'm right.' Defuse this self-centred tendency by asking for as many viewpoints as possible. Finding out what others think won't make you wrong; it will broaden your vistas.**

Broaden your vistas it will. But there are times when emotional control comes easier than others, right?

Part of leading under pressure is staying in emotional control. If you're in emotional control, you can create behavioural control. With behavioural control comes situational control.

Yes, it all starts with emotional control, and not going nuts in the moment, only to be sorry later for what you said or did. Your team needs you to keep it together. They're relying on you for the example of how to behave. And they need to know that you'll remain calm under fire, and that you have the ability to take charge of the situation or circumstance with control, care factor, and courage.

And, from our training and coaching programs, what we know works is:

BREATHE THROUGH IT.

You'll be amazed at how powerful your breath is for helping you stay in control. Yogis have known it for centuries, and we've finally cottoned on. Control your breathing, control your response.

BE STILL AND BE UNSPOKEN.

Don't feel like you have to say something in the moment. Take a second or ten (and even better, count backwards) to help you collect your thoughts and your emotions before you do anything.

BECOME SELF-AWARE AND PREPARED.

Know what your triggers are, and prepare for how you'll respond when you're triggered emotionally. If you're unprepared, and you're trigged anyway, revert to the two points above.

Your ability to create conscious control influences everything you do as a leader—and it can become an enduring trait or state that can help you to consistently lead well into the future, come what may.

THE 7 TRAITS AND STATES

In the last section, I unpacked the concept of leadership mandates (values alignment, transformational leadership, and created conscious control). These are critical elements of leadership, and they aren't skills as much as they're a way of being. A way of leading.

Specific leadership skills are either traits or states. Traits are characteristic patterns of thinking, feeling, and behaving that are adopted by leaders in general terms, in most situations; they differ between individuals and remain rather stable across time. States are characteristic patterns of thinking, feeling, and behaving in a specific situation at a particular moment in time. Traits are longer-term, and consistent. States (like moods) are more shorter-term and can vary.

Understanding the seven traits and states, and doing an inventory check on both, helps to develop an action plan based on the specific areas the leader wishes to work on—and to develop conscious control.

The 7 traits and states include:

ONE LEARNING.

Leaders are learners. The best leaders are constantly updating their knowledge base. They're learning about themselves and others. And they're learning about leadership. They're watching TED talks, they're reading books, they're listening to Podcasts or audiobooks, or they're studying a degree or similar.

Learning (growth) is a key human requirement. A human need. It's hard to continue to develop your leadership and your conscious control if you aren't learning new skills and knowledge on a regular basis. There's so much great information out there; it's just a matter of finding it.

TWO ENGAGING.

Engagement is a key leadership skill. Being engaging, and being interested, not interesting. Engaging others in conversations: caring conversations, robust conversations, career conversations. Communicating with others, in their style (DiSC), not your own.

Engaging leaders can hold the space when others need them to. They're emotionally intelligent, and they can think fast and talk slow. They understand what other people are feeling and experiencing. Engagement is about caring and connection, and it's underpinned by conscious control.

THREE ARTICULATING.

Leaders need to be able to give clear direction. Being able to articulate things like why you're a leader, what your leadership values are, and how they drive your behaviour, is a key leadership skill. To articulate what the vision, mission and values of the team are, and what the leader's expectations are. What the consequences of not meeting expectations will be, and why. You can't articulate properly without conscious control.

FOUR DEMONSTRATION.

Demonstration is about leading by example, and leading with integrity. Leading by example is not the most important thing about leadership: it's the ONLY thing that really matters.

Your team don't listen to you as much as they watch you, so remember that your behaviour is always on show. And be cognisant of what it's saying about you. It's important to have conscious control, because others follow your lead. If you ever wonder why your team is behaving in a certain way, always reflect on what you did or didn't do to encourage that behaviour, either consciously or subconsciously.

FIVE EMPATHY.

Empathy sits somewhere between apathy and sympathy. And it's really neither of these emotional states. Apathy is not caring, and sympathy is over-caring. Empathy is understanding, it's not about caring. Empathising is about walking in another person's shoes and understanding from a cognitive perspective what that situation must be like for the other person. It's about having the conscious control to take time to understand the other person's feelings, and being compassionate (which is about taking action of some sort to support the other person, if they need it).

SIX RESILIENCE.

There are six elements of resilience (the PR6, as developed by Jurie Rossouw),[21] and they include vision, collaboration, composure, health, tenacity, and reasoning.

Resilience is not about being able to cope with a tough situation. It's about advancing despite adversity. And you don't build resilience during a tough situation, you develop it before the situation. Or following it. Learning resilience before you need it is about personal development. Learning it following a tough situation can be part of post-traumatic growth (PTG). That way, when the same situation happens again, you'll be ready and better prepared to deal with it.

SEVEN SAFETY.

Your team members need to feel safe. Team members who feel safe will share their ideas, opinions, and views, and they don't have to worry about ridicule, rejection or resentment. Safety is a value, and it's about both feeling safe and working safely. Putting something else (like production, schedule, cost, or even your own feelings) above it could lead to dire consequences.

You're dealing with humans. That's why you need to have conscious control. You're not just dealing with your feelings; you're dealing with other people's—and some of them aren't dealing with theirs the way they should.

DEALING WITH BULLIES IN BUSINESS SUITS

Corporate bullying is an issue in Australia. HRM Solutions (and Safe Work Australia—SWA) has found that Australia has the sixth-highest rate of workplace bullying when compared with thirty-four European countries. According to SWA, the national average rate of workplace bullying has increased by 40%. This is supported by independent research conducted by the mental health charity, Beyond Blue, who suggest that almost 50% of all working Australians will experience bullying at some time in their work life.

Recently, and given my work as a leadership coach, I have done some radio interviews on bullies in business suits (see my post here). Yes, my focus is on working with leaders, those that do bully, and those that don't (depending on the situation). It's to help leaders refine their leadership skills and their ability to have a positive influence on their teams and their businesses. My purpose is to help leaders become better humans, and to create high-performing teams.

We do a lot of work in a coaching environment on leading organisations that don't tolerate bullying, and on helping bullying leaders to understand the impact they have on others. Unsurprisingly, it involves conscious control.

We also teach these skills in how to deal with a leader who's a bully.

ONE ORGANISATIONS NEED TO TAKE THE LEAD & MAKE CHANGE.

And they are.

Bullies in business suits usually promote or create what are known as 'toxic cultures.' Recently, an MIT Sloan Management Review study detailed that the main reason that staff are leaving organisations, as part of the great resignation, is due to a toxic culture. The study explains that the leading elements contributing to toxic cultures include failure to promote diversity, equity, and inclusion; workers feeling disrespected; and unethical behaviour.

Some organisations (and industries) still appear to accept these cultures as normal or OK. Recently, Hello Care reported on the thirty-five staff who were suspended, resigned, or were on stress leave amid bullying at an Adelaide aged care home, and the current and former employees told *The Advertiser* that a 'toxic' work culture was to blame.

The impact of toxic cultures (and bullying) is significant, but that's a topic for another book.

On the other side of the ledger, people-centred organisations like James Hardie (2022) and Cleanaway (2020) are looking at their senior leader behaviour and addressing the cultures in their businesses with programs like executive leadership mentoring, enhanced reporting, and monitoring of the leader's conduct. Yes, corporate Australia is taking a stand, and it's refreshing to see corporate culture turnarounds like these.

My prediction is that there will be more of these examples moving forward.

TWO TEAM MEMBERS AND STAFF NEED TO TAKE A STAND.

And they are.

Working for a bully is crippling. I've witnessed firsthand how much damage workplace bullying can do to team members. And I've been bullied in the workplace myself—which is one of the origin stories that drives the work that I do now.

The sad part is that it's hard to stand up to bullies. In my experience, they get louder, and more aggressive, more abusive, or more abrupt. But you must say something. You need to take a stand. You need to put your emotional and psychological safety first.

There are some very specific ways that you can have robust conversations with bullies in business suits, and create behavioural boundaries with a shared understanding of what you'll accept and tolerate as a team member. Be strong. Your mental health depends on it. Do this by calling attention to their values (or the organisational values) and share that bullying hurts people, and that if they value being a good human, bullying doesn't fit into that value system. Explain exactly how the bullying makes you feel, and the impact that it's having on you and/or your team. Finally, make it personal, by using the person's name a lot in the conversation. Try 'Jane, I get that you're under pressure, but Jane, I need you to stop (be specific here) because the impact is (be specific here). I treat you with respect, Jane, and I really need you to respect me too.'

THREE IF YOU'RE A BYSTANDER, IT'S YOUR TIME TO SHINE.

This paragraph is perhaps the most important part of this section.

One of the main reasons that bullying continues (unchecked) in organisations is due to what organisational psychologists call the 'Bystander Effect'. Britannica defines the Bystander Effect as 'the inhibiting influence of the presence of others on a person's willingness to help someone in need'. Research has shown that, even in an emergency, a bystander is less likely to extend help when he or she is in the real or imagined presence of others than when he or she is alone. In other words, humans are afraid to take a stand to help others in need—when other people are around and watching.

But we also know that bystanders are in the perfect position from which to act. They're witness to the poor behaviour, and they're not impacted personally, which means they can remain unbiased in the situation. They can generally keep their emotions in check, and they can be objective.

Bystanders, we need you! And I'm hoping as you read this that you don't need to help someone in your organisation or team who's being bullied. But if you do, don't miss the opportunity to call out the bullying. You might just be part of the solution, and help change a toxic work culture.

If your business has a toxic culture, or you're witnessing or experiencing workplace bullying, you can refer to the Safe Work Australia Guide to Preventing and Responding to Workplace Bullying.[23] You can also work with us at the Guinea Group to learn conscious control—one of the major safeguards against bullying behaviour.

DOES LEADERSHIP TRAINING REALLY WORK?

It sure does. And we've received too many positive testimonials and thank you messages following our programs to think any differently. And it's probably not even a matter of if leadership training works—it's a matter of what makes it work.

Let's unpack that.

ONE THE SETUP IS IMPORTANT.

The most important thing that a business can do prior to sending people to our programs is to let the attendees know what they're coming to, and why. Set them up for success. Too many times, in my last seventeen years of doing this, have I seen people turn up because there was an event in their calendar, but they had no idea what they were coming along to. Uncool.

We work with out clients, now, to make sure that never happens.

And it worked for one of our attendees. A few days before the program, we got a call to ask if he really need to come along. We mentioned that it could help his leadership. 'I've been a leader for thirty years,' he said, 'And I didn't even know leadership training was a thing.' He had a great time and learnt a lot, which his team now benefits from.

TWO THE TRAINER IS IMPORTANT.

We have a lot of trainees come through our programs, who have a very good 'BS-Meter'. In other words, they're cynical, they're potentially a little closed off, and they don't know if they'll get value from the time they invest into their own personal development.

This is where the quality of the trainer is vital. The trainer needs to be able to work with different learning styles, different communication styles, and different leadership styles. The trainer needs a high level of understanding in psychology and personality traits, and needs to be able to read a room, read humans, and read energy levels. They also need to be able to read a DiSC profile, to help leaders understand themselves and others.

THREE THE TRAINING IS IMPORTANT.

If you remember nothing else from this message, please remember that leadership training needs to be tailored to the audience, and to the attendees. Please don't book an off the shelf (vanilla) program for your team, then wonder why it didn't hit the mark.

When you're organising leadership training—please, please, please—tailor the training. So that you get feedback like this:

> **I would like to express a personal thank you for the training you delivered. It was not only interesting and valid, but I now have a better insight into the emotional side of the way we cope differently under pressure. This will assist me with the way I approach a situation and respond to gain the desired result with all stakeholders.**

So does leadership training work? If it's done right, and with the right approach—which entails a great deal of personal development, in creating the conscious control you need to lead your team in the right direction.

SO YOU WANT TO LOOK MORE PROFESSIONAL AS A LEADER

So you want to be able to lead your team in the right direction. But if you sometimes feel like you appear to be less professional than you could or should, this section is for you.

But what does it mean to look more professional? How do you do that, and why is it important?

This is an easy one. Looking professional means looking like you're in control. Did I say that? Yes. Being professional is another word for appearing to 'have it together', and to be leading on purpose. And with conscious control. So how do you look more professional?

Here are my three top tips, for looking like a professional in control.

ONE BE PREPARED FOR PRESENTATIONS OR MEETINGS.

Too many leaders think it's OK to 'wing it' or turn up without having done the pre-reading or the pre-thinking. And a little tip here: as leaders we expect our teams (and even our leaders) to do the prep prior to meetings, but there are times when we're found wanting on this one. This is seriously low-hanging fruit, and it can help you look professional with very little effort.

TWO THINK ABOUT FIRST IMPRESSIONS.

Think about what your office space says about you. And think about the messaging it sends to your team, or your clients. Especially when they visit to chat about high-value proposals. Paint the walls, put pictures up, buy some new chairs, make your space inviting. If you build it, they will come... and you'll look professional.

THREE FOCUS ON YOUR PERSONAL PRESENTATION.

And if you think this one isn't absolutely mission critical, think again. How you dress and how you present to your team daily tells people all they need to know about you. If you want to look professional, either dress professionally, or groom professionally (preferably both).

But WHY do you want to look more professional? Put simply, if you look more professional, you'll feel more professional. And if you feel more professional, you'll most likely act more professionally. Even deeper than that, looking more professional is a symbol. It says that you care. You care about yourself, you care about how you're perceived (yes, this matters), and you care about your team.

In a nutshell, if you want to look and be professional, you have to create conscious control. It's how you're going to deal with whatever comes your way, without harming anyone, even when you're still learning.

HOW TO FACE IT (NOT FAKE IT) UNTIL YOU MAKE IT

I'm just not a big fan of faking it. I've had to in the past, for sure, but I would much rather do the prep. Do the work. Do the thinking. And then, I'll get up, dress up, and show up. And yes, sometimes fail. And other times shine. It'll be a lesson or a blessing. The challenge for me with faking it is that impostor syndrome eventually shows up (thanks for that research, Carl

Jung), and it impacts my belief system about what I'm capable of.

Conversely, if I face up to what's happening, and get it done, even if it scares the you-know-what out of me, I'll give myself every chance to succeed.

But what does that take? It takes conscious control, and courage. Leadership courage is a central theme of our leading under pressure model, and we teach leaders the skills of having the courage to try, trust, and tell.

Did you know, though, that there are actually four types of courage? They were first unpacked by two researchers Pury and Lopez in 2010,[13] and since then, their model has been refined by authors like Cathy J Lassiter (in 2017).[13] The four types of courage include moral, disciplined, intellectual, and empathetic courage.

Let's look at these, and at how you, as a leader, can step into action by adopting one of these types of courage.

ONE MORAL COURAGE.

This is the courage that you need to stand up to injustice. To stand up when things are done that are immoral, unethical, or illegal. Think bullying. Think about being a bystander, and think about what it would take for you to say something. Standing up to things that aren't right does take courage—and getting over the fear of the outcome or the reaction of the human whose behaviour you're challenging. This is the courage that organisations are now legally obliged to support, some with a formal whistle-blower policy, to make it easier to speak up against inappropriate behaviour or poor treatment of others.

LEADER ACTION

As a leader, it's your responsibility to have this courage, and to take a stand again behaviour that violates the concept of being a good human. Regardless of the consequences. Regardless of whether the behaviour is being perpetrated at higher or lower levels of the organisation than you currently work at. To have this courage, think about the person who's being hurt, and how much they need your help and support.

TWO DISCIPLINED COURAGE.

This is the courage that you need to stand up for your position. To stand up when things are going badly. When you're losing faith. Or when others are losing faith in you.

And it would be easier to quit, right now, and give it all away. To leave the business, or to take another course of action that means you don't have to follow through on what you committed to, or that you know will be good for you or the business. This is the idea you had, or the project that you started on. Or the team that you took on, that isn't performing. Discipline and the courage to persevere will get you over a lot of hurdles. Note that this courage is akin to being resilient.

LEADER ACTION

As a leader, it's your responsibility to have this courage, and to take a stand for what you commit to doing. And to not giving in easily. Yes, that's easier said than done, but it's the tenacity that you started the project with that you'll need to call on when the challenges show up. Which they will. Have a vision. Know your end goal, and know that challenges are only temporary, and they're there to test your resolve.

THREE INTELLECTUAL COURAGE.

This is the courage that you need to turn your knowledge into action. To go out and learn something, and then apply that knowledge. It's the courage to contribute at a higher level. It's the courage to take a research report, or a blog, and value the information enough to apply it to your leadership style. It's the courage to train others in it, because this new knowledge is important, and worthwhile. And it's about learning from your experience and applying those learnings to get better outcomes into the future.

LEADER ACTION

As a leader, it's your responsibility to have this courage, and to learn new things. Yes, leaders are learners. And without the commitment to learning new knowledge and skills, it's hard to apply anything new or to try something different. Secondly, intelligently courageous leaders challenge the norms. They're willing to back themselves to get a different result, through a new approach and a new strategy, as much as others might push back at the time. Which will happen. Leaders that get good at rejection, get good at resilience.

FOUR EMPATHETIC COURAGE.

My favourite form of courage. Love this one. We train leaders in this type of courage more than anything else. Empathy is an important leadership skill, but yes, it takes courage to implement.

Empathetic courage is about being aware enough of your personal biases and challenging them, so that you're better placed to vicariously experience what others are going through and to understand why. It's about being the person that can understand the trials and tribulations of others, without being exclusive or judgemental. Empathy is a cognitive, emotional, and compassionate process (Credit: Daniel Goleman)[ii] where we look to think about and feel what others are experiencing, so that we can be there to include, support, or to care for them, as required.

LEADER ACTION

As a leader, it's your responsibility to have this courage, and to know that another person's experience is their experience, is their reality, and is important or even life-changing for them. Just because you 'judge' it to be less than important or relevant, leaders need to step into their empathetic selves (fun fact: we were all born with compassion, we just forget it sometimes). And they need to hold the space so that the impacted person can talk and share in a safe space that is free from ridicule, resentment, or rejection. This is deep courage, and courage that has the potential to change lives. It's that important.

As a leader, you should adopt the four types of courage, and face up to the things that cause you to be fearful. Drawing on courage, and applying the principles of conscious control, will help you not only face up but to deal with problems in a way that helps, not hurts, your team.

ACTIVITY 2.1
CREATE CONSCIOUS CONTROL

Take some time now to think about what you've learnt in the last chapter.

The series of questions on the following pages will encourage you to think about ways you can improve your conscious control, and how you can apply the lessons you've just learnt in the process of upskilling your leadership.

If you find this activity doesn't work for you, consider journalling. It's also a valuable use of time just to sit and write about your values, your goals, and any challenges you need to tackle in your leadership role.

What could you do to create conscious control, to avoid reacting and start responding in effective ways?

In what ways could you take a stand against bullying in your workplace?

List ways you could more effectively support team members who are taking a stand against bullying in your workplace.

Are you confident in your ability to stand up to injustice?

What personal presentation issues could you improve to present better as a competent but approachable leader?

What tasks or projects have you not followed through on? And what can you do to be more disciplined in the future?

What could you start learning now to gain more knowledge and be a more confident leader in your field?

What personal biases do you need to confront and challenge to be a better leader?

SKILL II

HAVE HIGH CARE FACTOR

THE CARE FACTOR STRATEGY FOR LEADERS

In 2020, John Mackey[ii] wrote the book Conscious Leadership. In that book (one of my faves), Mackey talked about how to use love, compassion, and human qualities to build the business *Whole Foods Market Service*. He also unpacked the nine elements of conscious leadership.

One review of the book reads:

> **Rarely does a book move me to tears, yet this one did, by holding up a mirror to the kind of leader I most deeply want to be. Conscious Leadership is a powerful invitation to shift our mindset from the win/lose games of war to the community-building virtues of love, authenticity, and integrity. It's a book built on the radical idea that business can be a force for bringing more love into the world. Count me in.**

For me, this book was next level. It talked about the power of love, and how a care factor approach to leadership can change a business and make a difference in society. Yes, it talked about vision and goals, and purpose and process, but the theme of the book was around how to be a great leader by leaning into being a great human.

Mackey unpacks how you can do this, using the three elements of Conscious Leadership (Vision and Virtue, Mindset and Strategy, People and Culture). Each one of these can be broken down into three key strategies.

Number one under vision and virtue is simply to 'Put People First.' It's a simple message. But how do you do that? You can read the book, or you can read on and get my take on it, and (like I always do) find the short cut or the simple way to explain and implement an important message.

ONE CARE FACTOR IS ABOUT TIME.

One of the things that leaders don't want to hear is that their team members feel that the leader doesn't care about them. It's not uncommon to hear this, and our coaching clients present with this challenge at times. Especially when the leader is busy, under pressure, or trying to juggle a lot of balls.

What it means when a team member says they don't feel cared for is that the leader doesn't give the team member (or the team) the time that they deserve. The leader is absent. The leader is preoccupied with everything other than their team.

The solution for this one is to find time in your calendar to be with your team members, and your team, whether that's 1:1 meetings or team meetings. Leaders who take the time to be present demonstrate a level of care factor for their team, and they're respected for it.

Giving time is about making a statement about what's important. When your team is important enough to get your time, your team members feel valued and cared for.

TWO CARE FACTOR IS ABOUT CONVERSATION.

And I don't mean one-way conversation. I mean conversing. And when a leader is conversing, what they should be doing is asking questions, and keeping the discussion moving. Learning about the team member.

The word converse comes from Middle English (in the sense 'live among, be familiar with'); from Old French, 'converser'; from Latin, 'conversari' ('keep company with'. Its meaning is also evident in its components: 'con-' means 'with', and 'versare', a frequentative of 'vertere', means 'to turn'. The current sense of the verb dates from the early seventeenth century (Credit: Oxford Languages Definitions).

Conversation is about connection. And as per the definition, it means to be familiar with team members. To turn towards team members. To keep company with them, with the right level of connection and direction.

But that's not enough practical information. Here's the conversation strategy you need:

- **Ask Psychological Safety questions.** Ask whether it's safe to share ideas, opinions, and views. Ask if it's safe to contribute at high levels, and ask if your team member feels safe to challenge the norms.

- **Ask Psychological Empowerment questions.** Ask whether your team members feel like they're having an impact. Are they getting meaning from their work? Do they feel like they have a sense of self-determination (ownership of their work choices), and do they feel competent to fulfill the duties of their role?

- **Ask Psychological Connection questions.** These questions are about career direction. This is where you learn not 'where' your team members want to be in five years, but 'what' they want to be doing. The 'what' is a better type of question, because when you know that you can look for the right opportunities to help the team member get there. All the while remembering that there are some team members who never want to do anything other than what they are doing now—which is important to understand. When you can converse in a way that is focused on connecting with your team members (and understanding their needs), your team members feel cared for.

THREE CARE FACTOR IS ABOUT COURAGE.

When it comes time to have a robust conversation, if the first two points have been addressed, this third point should take care of itself.

I couldn't tell you how many leaders avoid the courageous conversations. They don't want to hurt the team member by delivering bad news. What they don't realise is that avoidance is ruinous. Avoiding courageous conversations does not help your team members, it harms them. And most of the time, the team member either knows it's being avoided, or would rather know than be kept in the dark.

Yes, these conversations take preparation. They take planning, and they take precision. They need to be handled correctly. When you can have courageous conversations with your team members to support their growth and development, your team members feel cared for.

What could you do today, to give time, to get connected, or to be courageous with your team?

HOW TO BE A GOOD HUMAN AND A GOOD LEADER

If you read the first book in this series, you'll have already read this story. But it's so important that it bears repeating, because you can learn a lot from the person I'm not proud to have once been.

I was not a nice human when I was younger. I was angry, had a log (not a chip) on both shoulders, and was very quick to escalate a conversation. From controlled to crazy out-of-control. Highly emotional. I had zero emotional intelligence, and I didn't care. At that time, anyway.

I was a tradie, so it didn't seem like a big deal that I was angry AF. Everyone was like that. Or were they? There weren't too many on my crew that had the lack of emotional control that I did.

But I made it OK. Until one day it just got out of control. I had a massive stand up blue in the workshop, with the boilermaker on our shift. It was so uncool! Let's just say that the language we used towards each other was pretty colourful.

My lovely wife remembers the conversation that evening, and it was about my baring my soul and being brutally honest about my lack of people skills. I don't remember the exact words I used, but Mrs G remembers me saying that I was sick of not being able to get on with people, and that I was totally committed to changing my approach. And to learning new skills. I just didn't have great communication skills.

And it meant that I wasn't a high-quality human. Why? Because my behaviour hurt others. It literally caused hurt.

So, I wanted to change. But where to start, in the elusive quest for better communication and connection with others, and to be a better human?

It started with study at Monash University, doing management, and then a HR degree and a post graduate diploma at CQU. That'll fix it, I thought. The study was useful, and so was the work that I was doing on trying to understand humans. Understanding others was about watching and listening. Looking and learning. What made people tick? And more importantly, what made them crack?

The journey has never stopped (and I feel like it's an ongoing mission). Recently, I completed a psychology degree. In saying that, the one qualification that was the best thing I ever studied was NLP (Neuro-Linguistic Programming), and love it or loathe it, that program was an eye opener into the human species and how we all connect. Having studied people for nearly thirty years (and now doing a PhD in behavioural science),

I share with leaders some of the simple techniques that they can use to improve their leadership and their connection. Especially when they're under pressure, which is the hardest time to connect. And the hardest time to be a good human.

Here's my take on what it takes to be a good human, and how care factor relates to leading under pressure. I'm still learning these skills, but here are some of the important things I've learnt to date

ONE DO NO HARM.

This is such a simple rule, but one that can easily be overlooked. Now, I get that most people will not go through their life without hurting someone. But it's still rule number one of being a good human.

What no harm means is subjective. In my words, it's simply: don't deliberately make someone feel bad. Don't deliberately denigrate. Don't communicate in a way that is aggressive, abusive, or abrupt. Which can happen when you're under emotional strain. You might lash out. Or you might not take the time to think about your impact on others. No one likes people that make them feel bad about themselves.

For leaders, what doing no harm means is being committed to doing leadership work in a way that's respectful. Regardless of whether you like a team member, whether or not they're in your in-group or out-group (yes, you categorise your team members), every team member deserves respect. Even when you're busy, or under pressure.

Yes, it takes time to be respectful. But yes, you can do no harm even when you're having robust conversations or delivering bad news. That is, if you plan the conversation and the information being delivered. Like being a good human, if you can remove aggression, abruptness, and abuse from your communication style, you'll do no harm. How do I know that? Because at least 75% of the DiSC profiles that I read say that the person will get put out if you're abrupt with them.

You really can do no harm if you're intentional about being respectful. It takes work, but it feels a lot better than ruminating about hurting others, if that ever happens. Do no harm!

TWO LEAVE PEOPLE BETTER THAN YOU FOUND THEM.

If you've ever been to one of our training programs, you'll have heard me say these words. Because it's my absolute purpose in life, and because it's the biggest learning to do that actually helps people have a better emotional experience, just by being around you. You can positively impact another human, even in the workplace.

Now, if you're willing to get a bit cosmic with me, you'll know that I believe every single human carries around an aura. An aura is emotionally charged. And your aura is contagious. Yes, contagious. So, in short, the happier you are, the happier those around you will be. Just by you being in their space. How big a space? The largest distance I've read is nine metres—that means that you have a nine-metre radius of energy that's impacting others (I did say it would be a bit cosmic).

So, now that you know you're influencing others with your emotional state, would it make sense to try and feel good so that others do in your presence? You know the old saying, 'they light up the room when they walk in.' That's because those people walk into the room happy. Plain and simple.

Let's go one step further and say that if you're going to influence others anyway, you might as well be intentional about it. You can, by managing your emotional state.

For leaders, what this means is to be positive. Or at least, more positive than you're negative. This is not about positive thinking, or sunshine or rainbows, but it's about things like using language that's uplifting, not putting down. The good thing about leadership is that you get to work on this over time, because you get to see your team members every day, and you can keep improving on this one.

When you're under pressure, that's the time when you're most likely to be direct. Negative. And angry. And that's the time that you will not leave people better than you found them. Try to be positive in your emotions and your language. Leave people better than you found them!

THREE LEARN MORE SO YOU CAN SHARE MORE.

This is such an underestimated skill for being a good human.

Some theory first (from the Tony Robbins playbook, at least) in relation to learning and growth. Tony Robbins's theory[20] is that the human species has two major human needs: to grow and to contribute. In theory, the more we grow and contribute, the happier we are in life. Great!

Let's take this a step further and consider how this theory could make you a good human. Because the more that you grow, the more you can contribute, right? If you stop learning, you stagnate, and your level of contribution remains the same. Until you start learning again.

To me, being a good human means working on yourself so that you can add more value to the planet, and you can share more with others. Share more knowledge, share deeper conversations, and even share more wealth (the more you learn, the more you earn). You see, the old adage of you can't help others until you can help yourself, and you need to fill your own cup first, is true. To a point. If you're filling your cup with knowledge of some sort. Even self-knowledge.

Some people say we're like trees. We're either green or brown, growing or dying. And there's some truth to this simple analogy.

For leaders, you'll experience learning during the first day of our programs (LEAD: learn, engage, articulate, demonstrate). Learn about yourself, learn about others, and learn about leadership. Learn more. Even just learn about why you do leadership. Most of the leaders that come through our programs can't explain why they do leadership. If the leader doesn't know why they do leadership, how will their teams know?

Learn more so you can share more.

Being a good human is an achievable goal. It takes effort, and care factor, and the best way to do it is to make it a priority. Make humans your priority, and watch your life and your leadership improve. Even when there are new challenges coming.

THE TOP 3 LEADERSHIP CHALLENGES IN THE 2020S AND BEYOND

These next years are going to be tough for leaders. They'll be fraught with challenges in the IT space, in the employee wellbeing space, and in the diversity and flexibility space. Leaders need to be ready to face these challenges and be equipped with the skills need to lead teams in the 2020s and beyond—primarily, the skill of care factor.

Here's how care factor looks different to what it looked like in the past.

ONE THE CHANGING IT LANDSCAPE.

The list of challenges in the IT space is long and difficult. From what software applications you should be using, to the implications of AI and VR for your business, to the risk of a cyberattack on your systems, IT's impact on your business needs to be considered.

But it also offers a lot for your growth as a leader. Applications like Noom or Calm will help you with your health and relaxation. You could also turn to AI, and Chat GPT, for advice on how to deal with certain situations.

Chat GPT is taking the world by storm right now, and rightly so. Some pundits are saying it'll challenge Google into the future. Or you could turn to VR and simulation to train your team members. But all of these take time, and take effort to learn them, right?

With new technology, it's generally a case of short-term pain for long-term gain. Apps are designed to save us time, but it just never feels like that, especially in the early days of adoption.

If you're running a consulting business, video marketing is king right now. Instagram feeds and TikTok videos are hot to reach the younger demographic. And Gary Vee predicted that Facebook reels will be the best way to connect with Gen X in the 2020s.

But even if you don't do any of the above, the one thing that you should be focused on is cyber security. With cyber crime becoming an accepted business model in the 2020s, it's important to care enough to protect your information, and your company's, so you don't end up paying a criminal to get access to your data.

TWO EMPLOYEE WELLBEING SHOULD BE A MAJOR FOCUS.

Last year, the Australian Government released the work-related psychological health and safety Systematic Approach to Meeting Your Duties.[22] The introduction to that document states that:

> **This Guide describes a systematic practical approach to managing work-related psychological health and safety. Most elements of this systematic approach are required under work health and safety (WHS) or workers' compensation laws in all Australian jurisdictions. This Guide recognises poor psychological work health and safety can lead to both psychological and physical injuries.[20]**

Yes, the psychological safety of our teams has always been important, but now it's moved from being a moral obligation to a legal one. Regulators will now be very interested in compliance with this guidance material, particularly if team members need leave to deal with mental health issues— if they're deemed to be caused by their workplace.

And rightly so. Good leaders understand the importance of psychological safety, and they'll already be doing a lot of what's in that guide. But if you're not adopting the requirements of that guide, you'll be leaving your organisation and team members exposed.

THREE DIVERSITY AND INCLUSION ARE NOW DIVERSITY AND FLEXIBILITY.

Diversity and inclusion have been front and centre for leaders for a long time now, but the last two years have seen a global change in how team members want to work. The workplace has moved from being accepting and inclusive (regardless of beliefs or sexual orientation, etc.) to having to balance a hybrid workforce.

Yes, diversity in decision making has always been seen as the best way to foster innovation and creativity. In the 2020s, though, leaders now need to try and maintain that flexibility, and maintain either a four-day work week, or a workforce that only comes into the office for one or two days a week.

There's data and reports detailing the best work rosters and the most flexible arrangements that promote productivity in work teams. But at the end of the day, leaders need to be all over not just that information, but also the administration and the rostering that flexibility requires. Because every team member is different, and what suits one team member may not necessarily suit another.

Leaders everywhere are in for a tough time in the 2020s, where they'll be challenged on all fronts. It might be time to consider getting a leadership coach, to support you in your commitment to being a leader who's remembered for the right reason—their care factor.

HOW TO BE THE LEADER THAT PEOPLE REMEMBER (FOR THE RIGHT REASONS)

I had some average leaders as I was climbing the ladder of corporate success. They're now called 'old-school leaders'. And I can remember them clearly, and what they said, and how they said it. I went into leadership coaching to see if I could help leaders like them to be better at leading humans—by leading them with care factor. So that teams everywhere didn't have the have the same experience that I had.

Sometimes, though, I have to reflect and remember that there have been some great leaders along the way, too. And I've learnt a heap from them. Particularly, if you've seen my origin story video, where I talk through an incident that occurred on a power station on May 21, 2021 where the leaders stepped up and stepped into leadership under pressure. In a way that was all about control, care factor and courage.

As well as that experience, at the start of our leadership training sessions, I used to take our attendees on a journey of thinking about their worst ever leader. The purpose of that session is to remember what it feels like when we're exposed to poor leadership, so we don't be a leader who's remembered for that reason.

We've changed that up now, because such a negative session (and it was negative) took the emotions in the wrong direction and I had to spend the next two days turning it around. Now, we talk about our favourite leaders of all time, and what they did that made them our favourite leaders. We put all those notes on a whiteboard, and essentially write the playbook for what great leadership looks like from a very personal experience. A much more positive session, sure.

Eventually, the focus turns to me, and the group asks me who my favourite leader has been, and why. So, I share my experience, and I'm very specific about why this person was my favourite leader.

Here's my contribution to that session.

ONE MY FAVOURITE LEADER WAS PATIENT, AND TOOK A COACHING APPROACH.

I worked for a year on a major commissioning project. A major plant expansion had been completed by a major construction company, and I was working with the owner's team on the commissioning element of the construction project. I was in a tough role (project controls), and it was detail, detail, detail. Schedules and numbers. Facts and figures. Progress and process. Not skills that I necessarily had at the time (I am high (I) influence on my DiSC profile, and very low (C) conscientious). I'm not a details person.

Within a year, I'd turned that around. For that year, I learnt to do data. I learnt to do numbers. With my leader's help.

I needed a significant amount of support and coaching. Once I got the hang of it, things got better. And at the end of the year, we started doing planning workshops that I could facilitate. Winner. Being in front of humans. Way more fun.

But I will never forget that leader, and I'll be forever grateful for the patience that he showed when he knew that detail was not a strong point of mine. I'm sure it was, but nothing ever seemed to be too much trouble for him; he always had time for me, and always spoke in a way that was encouraging and not demeaning. I appreciated that.

One thing I remember clearly was the day that that leader asked for a rewrite of the commissioning plan...in an hour...with a heap of changes. I freaked out. He was patient. He said something like: 'I know what I've asked for is one or more days' work. But I have to present something to my leader in an hour, so I need your best effort for an hour, with complete focus. I gave you an hour, and I need a great hour. Then we can finish it off.' So, I went nuts for an hour, and nailed as much as I could. Which wasn't much, but it was enough.

After that, the coaching started, and he helped me through the document rewrite, in a coaching way. It was like that leader really knew how to work under pressure. It seemed to come naturally, though I feel like this might actually have been learnt behaviour. Regardless, it was an amazing skill. Patience and coaching.

TWO MY FAVOURITE LEADER WAS AN INTROVERT, IN AN EXTROVERT'S ROLE.

This was a revelation for me at that time. There was a period in my life where I was convinced that only extroverts made good leaders. How wrong I was.

Because this leader was such a coach for me, I was able to get an insight into his personality. And I was able to see the quiet times, not just the times that he was in front other others. As an example, that leader would go from being in front of his team, looking like an extrovert, to his office, slouched in his chair recovering from all the people interactions.

He explained that he was highly introverted, and that doing people work was a huge energy drainer for him. He needed time alone to get his energy back, and recharge, before going an doing it all again, for the rest of the day.

It was like that leader had this complete understanding of self, and was totally aware of his strengths and weaknesses. He knew when and how to step up and step into people interactions, even when he didn't feel like it was his skill set. Interestingly, if you asked people about him, they would have thought he was very extroverted. But he wasn't. He was an introvert, in an extrovert's role.

THREE MY FAVOURITE LEADER ACTUALLY CARED ABOUT PEOPLE.

This is an interesting point, because there are leaders who try to care, but struggle to. There are leaders who are very clear on the fact that they don't care as much about people as they do about the process or the output.

One day, I got a call to say my son had been rushed to hospital after falling off his skateboard and bashing his head on the bitumen. He was wearing a helmet, thankfully, but I didn't know that until I got to the hospital.

This leader could not do enough to support and look after me that day, and that week. Time off was not an issue, leaving quickly was fine, and he gave me a lift around town to pick up my car from site and get my son from hospital to home. It was next level care. And I appreciated it.

It was like that leader knew how to care. And it didn't seem like any effort at all. It seemed to be important to that leader, to care for people.

FYI, it's a much better way to start a session, asking about people's favourite leader, and not their worst. And it's nice to be able to share the above reflections with my attendees. Fun fact: I remember that leader for all the right reasons—which were all care factor. You can't lead well without it.

YOU AREN'T LEADING IF YOU AREN'T DOING THIS ONE THING

The biggest challenge leaders have is that they need to give so much of themselves to others. Leaders need to constantly show up, with purpose, with passion, and with persistence. They need to be there to coach, to counsel, and to collaborate. With care factor.

Which can be difficult at times, especially when there are people in your team that are having struggles that affect their work and their focus. And the leader may not be able to understand why those issues are such a big deal. But they are, for that person.

When your team members are struggling, your leadership skills will be on show. And they'll be tested. Because you need to step into their shoes and demonstrate care factor. And compassion.

I'm going to make a big call in this section and say that if you don't know how to be compassionate, or you're choosing not to be compassionate, you're not being the best leader you can be.

Here's why.

ONE COMPASSION IS MISUNDERSTOOD.

Compassion literally means 'to suffer together'. Among emotions researchers, it's defined as the feeling that arises when you're confronted with another's suffering, and feel motivated to relieve that suffering. Compassion is not the same as empathy or altruism, though the concepts are related. (Credit: Greatergood.com)

Compassion is a two-stage process, firstly involving understanding, then secondly acting. There is no compassion without action. You must take an action if you're being compassionate. That action might be as simple as listening. It might be providing compassionate leave, if someone is dealing with loss or grief. It might be making someone a coffee, or it might be driving them to a psychologist.

Our cat died recently, and for some non-cat lovers, that wouldn't mean much. My wife Julie, though, was shattered. More than shattered. And nearly didn't go to work for the day (my son took the day off—our cat was beloved). Most people would not be able to understand that. One of Julie's friends found a photo of our cat (with Julie) and got it put on a key ring as a reminder. Julie didn't know about it, and it made her day. That's compassion—action that matters.

LEADER ACTION

Don't assume you know what the person needs you to do, as compassionate action. There are times when you'll just have to follow your instincts.

TWO MOST PEOPLE ARE BORN COMPASSIONATE.

In baby studies, compassion shows up at about the eight-month mark. Research with eight-month-old babies showed that when one of them was in distress, the others took action so their mate got help more quickly.

Babies have also been found to cry in response to another newborn baby's cry, which psychologists agree are early signs of the development of compassion. Studies have shown that when a baby hears another baby crying, their sucking motion and heart rate slow in response to the sound. They have a physical reaction to the distress that they're hearing. This is a natural response. And here's the kicker: studies have found that a small percentage of newborns don't react like that—which might predict a lack of compassion as the child grows.

It's generally thought that compassion proper begins to show itself in the second year of life. But it could be there a lot earlier. In other words, the vast majority of humans are born compassionate.

LEADER ACTION

If you're a leader struggling with compassion, that's a nurture thing, not a nature thing. You've either forgotten or not chosen compassion. If you're struggling with it, know it's a skill that you most likely possess, and it just takes some willingness and time to get better at it.

THREE COMPASSION IS NOT SYMPATHY.

Compassion is an element of empathy, says Daniel Goleman[II] in his literature around emotional intelligence. And sadly, most people think empathy is sympathy, which is feeling sorry for someone and crying or hurting for them.

Think of a scale for a minute, with sympathy at one end, and apathy at the other. Both of these are natural emotional states. If someone is in pain, you either feel for them, or you're apathetic (you don't care at all)—there is very little in between. Either high care factor or low care factor.

The challenge with compassion (or substitute that with empathy for this section), you need to understand which natural response you've just experienced, and then move from that to understanding (cognitively and emotionally) so that you can be empathetic. Empathy is an action (as above), not a feeling.

If you're not compassionate and empathetic right now, the good news is that it's a learnt skill. It's something that you can practice.

LEADER ACTION

Prepare for conversations that you might need to have with team members who are hurting. And use words or phrases like 'talk me through it', or 'help me understand', or 'that must be tough'. Please don't start with 'I understand', especially if you don't.

You're not leading (and certainly not leading well), if you're not being compassionate when it matters. Care factor matters. It's how you lead well, in the face of pressure and new industry challenges.

HOW TO NAVIGATE THE CHALLENGES OF LEADERSHIP IN HEAVY INDUSTRY

Leadership can be tough at the best of times. But when you add in an old-school culture, changing technology, and a diverse workforce, leadership gets even harder. This is what leaders in heavy industry are faced with. The last five to ten years has seen unprecedented change in heavy industrial organisations and teams.

The question is, how do you navigate these challenges, and continue to develop your leadership skills, amid the change?

Having a mix of corporate and heavy industry clients, I can see what happens in both worlds and how they differ. For our heavy industry leaders, these are the clients I see having to learn the most and adapt the most.

OLD SCHOOL CULTURE AND BOYS' CLUBS ARE ON THEIR WAY OUT

This is the big one. The new-age leadership style is here, and it's here to stay. We're not going back to the shouting or swearing at each other. Or back to telling inappropriate jokes, or to having naked posters in crib rooms, or to being offensive to other humans.

Yes, there is an expectation of leaders (and workers) in the 2020s, that they'll adapt to the new normal of the new workplace. Where it's easy to be offensive, and leaders need to understand that. They need to change their languaging and their behaviour. They need to develop emotional intelligence. For some, with forty or fifty years of heavy industry experience, this is proving difficult. Rightly so. It's a massive change.

Some people might term this section 'political correctness', and they might even follow that up with 'has gone mad'. I'm OK with political correctness, because it makes us all learn how to be better humans, and not offend others (intentionally or unintentionally).

My experience is that some leaders are holding on to the old school, but most are trying to adapt. And congratulations to them, as their teams and organisations are the beneficiaries of their growth and upgraded skills.

If you're reading this, and you want to make some changes, reach out to us, or do some work on your conversational skills and emotional intelligence. They're great places to start.

TECHNOLOGY IS NOT GOING ANYWHERE

This is perhaps the biggest challenge for heavy industry. It appears to be being embraced well. Or at least to the point where leaders know what technology they need to utilise, and they go and get some training or some instruction on how to do it.

One thing about technology is that it's getting easier to use. Whether it's remote equipment operating technology or messaging apps on a phone, the interaction element of technology has taken massive leaps forward in recent years, to the benefit of workplaces across every industry. For senior leaders, the biggest challenge remains in the cyber security space, with hacker attacks being a very real risk.

For me, technology is such a big part of our lives that I feel like it shouldn't rate as a key challenge for heavy industry leaders. But I still hear some of the challenges that leaders face during coaching sessions.

I only ever have one piece of coaching advice for leaders struggling with technology, and that's to get through the fear of learning something new, and jump in. Do what it takes to learn the technology or software as quickly as you can, and move onto the next one.

WORKFORCES ARE BECOMING MORE AND MORE DIVERSE

Heavy industry is becoming more diverse by the day. Which is great, as people shouldn't be discriminated against because of something about them that doesn't affect how well they can perform their work.

Referring to point one, where a lot of leaders (and workers) are old school, having an Indigenous person, a transgender person, or anyone from the LGBTIQA+ community for that matter, can be a challenge. But why? Why do some people struggle with people who are different from the majority?

It's a challenge because it's so different to how a lot of people in heavy industry were raised (me included). But if you can reframe the situation, and realise that everyone is just another human—someone to engage with and learn from—it really can be that simple. No need to complicate it.

Having said that, there are a range of peripheral challenges that come with diverse workforces, including toileting access. But none of these challenges are insurmountable. If you're engaging with and learning from your people with human-centred acceptance, you can be a better leader in leading diverse workforces.

Old school is out. And technology and diversity are in. And these changes need care factor, which is challenging for some leaders in heavy industry.

As a closing comment, I was part of a conversation recently, where I was advocating for more progressive leadership thinking. The person I was talking about was an ally (and worked on a heavy industrial site with about a thousand people). The conversation ended with the statement from that person to the effect of 'the best thing that could happen to our outdated workforce is for us to hire a transgender or other minority group person, so that everyone has to learn to be accepting.' Well said, I thought.

ACTIVITY 2.2
HAVE HIGH CARE FACTOR

Take some time now to think about what you've learnt in the last chapter.

The series of questions on the following pages will encourage you to think about what you can do to have high care factor, and how you can apply the lessons you've just learnt in the process of upskilling your leadership.

Alternatively, consider journalling. It's also an effective way to learn more about being a good human as well as a good leader, and to develop strategies to become the leader that people remember for the right reasons—for your care factor, even when you're under pressure.

What are some of the biggest challenges in your workplace as it moves into a more inclusive future?

What could you do to create more time in your calendar to support your team members?

Do you think your team members feel safe to share their ideas, opinions, and views? Why, or why not?

Do you think your team members feel like their work has an impact in the organisation? Why, or why not?

What opportunities could you provide for your team members who want to upgrade their skill sets or progress their careers?

Answer honestly. Are you 'doing no harm' to your team members?

Are you engaged in learning to share knowledge? If not, what could you learn that you could share?

What could you do to improve your focus on your employees' wellbeing?

What changes could you make in your workplace to create an environment to make it more supportive of diversity and inclusion?

Note some characteristics of leaders you admire the most, and how you could emulate them.

SKILL III
DEVELOP YOUR EMOTIONAL QUOTIENT

WHY EI MATTERS

In the 2020s, your Emotional Intelligence (EI or EQ) matters. Daniel Goleman[i] argues that in leadership positions, 85% of the competencies for success lie in the EI domain, rather than in technical or intellectual abilities.

With that in mind, what is it that you can do to develop your emotional intelligence? The answer: a lot.

There really are a range of tools that you can add to your toolbox that will allow you to stay in emotional control while building rapport with other humans. And although we've been doing training in the EI domain for many years, we're finally able to give you an accurate read on your level of EI. As part of our DiSC profiling work, we now have a profiling tool that not only helps you unpack your EI, but helps you to improve it.

And why is that important? Because without EI, the quality of your own emotional experience, and the emotional experiences of those around you, won't be as good as they could, and the relationships you have with yourself and others will suffer. Better EI means better emotional state, and better connections with other humans.

What I love about the profiling tool is that it follows the Daniel Goleman[i] model of self-recognition and self-management, and social-recognition and social-management. For most people that I speak to, it's the social-management element of the EI model that is important.

Let me add as much value as I can by sharing the top five skills of those that are high EI, and that are great at social management (relationships). These these are taken from the EI profiling tool.

EMPATHY, SENSITIVITY, APPRECIATION.

This skill is about understanding others—accurately picking up emotional cues from communication (including words, tone, and nonverbal signals);

managing direct and indirect feedback effectively; and being attentive, sensitive, aware, and appreciative of the emotional signals of others.

SERVICE, COMPASSION, BENEVOLENCE.

This skill is about operating with a sense of contribution. Aiding, helping, coaching, and developing others; operating constructively to contribute to the emotional states and benefits of others; recognising needs, wants and desires; and relating to alternative thoughts, perceptions, and perspectives.

HOLISTIC COMMUNICATION.

This skill is about having the ability to effectively send and receive information including emotional content. It involves listening; engaging and connecting with others; and sending and receiving verbal and nonverbal signals constructively.

SITUATIONAL PERCEPTUAL AWARENESS.

This skill is about recognising and processing dynamic, shifting emotional data. Communicating attention, focus, awareness, and connection; adapting to situational variables and changes; understanding which factors count, and how much; and responding with reasonable behaviour.

INTERPERSONAL DEVELOPMENT.

This skill is about growing and nurturing constructive connections. It's about setting the tone for long-term depth and breadth in relationships; working with quality in personal and professional relations; and having resonance and rapport with others.

Looking at the list, it's clear how these skills can help you be more successful, not only at work, but also out of work. These are life skills that increase the quality of your life, by increasing your emotional quotient, for higher quality interactions with others that are consistent across time.

EMOTIONAL CONSISTENCY IS NOT EMOTIONAL SUPPRESSION

If I was to do a straw poll of our coaching clients, and I asked them the one thing that they value in their leader, one common answer would be (and yes, we have asked) emotional consistency. Or a derivation of such.

And what I interpret this as meaning is not only emotional consistency, but also behavioural consistency. In short, and from your team's perspective, all they want is that the same leader shows up every day (or at least most days). Leaders that are all over the place create teams that are all over the place. A client told me recently that they didn't know which version of their leader they were getting each day. And that is seriously uncool from a leadership perspective.

BUT WHAT IS EMOTIONAL CONSISTENCY?

Great question, and I think it's important to acknowledge that leadership is emotional work, and it challenges us daily to stay consistent and in control. Given that, emotional control isn't about avoiding the crappy emotions. It's about not lashing out with venom and hurting others because you've just gotten bad news or because your world has gone BOOM.

From a psychological perspective, humans can't know what light is without dark. We can't know happiness without sadness. Humans can only have an experience, or an emotion, if we have a contrast or something to compare it to. So, positive emotions are only possible because we have the not-so-positive emotions. In the moments of not-so-positive, don't suppress your emotions. Reframe them, and channel them for good.

Find that way inside yourself to switch your thinking and feeling so that your emotional state, whatever it is, helps others. Not hurts them. Heals others, not harms them. If you need some support or tips on this, please reach out at anton@theguineagroup.com.au.

In short, great leadership is about predictable leadership. Consistent leadership. That's the easiest way to say it, really. Don't be a tornado or a hurricane. Be a gentle breeze that has a cooling effect, instead of a catastrophic natural disaster effect.

To unpack emotional control differently—and just off topic for a paragraph—I read a lot of books, and I reach out to the authors when I finish them. One author, Sky Nelson-Isaacs[17] (author of the book Living in Flow) explained it beautifully in a LinkedIn message reply, where he shared:

> I'm very keen on the journey of controlling emotions. Not silencing them, mind you, but channelling them to the right output, so that we can stay in flow. When we suppress emotions, our equilibrium starts to shift, so eventually we need to blow off steam. Good leaders under pressure can transmute those difficult emotions into caring and loving emotions and stay top of their game.

And I think that sums up emotional control. And why it's not emotional suppression. It's about emotional channelling, to use our emotions—

regardless of what we're experiencing as leaders—for good.

With emotional control comes behavioural control, and comes situational control. And with that comes a high-performing team, who aren't freaking out about how their leader will respond if they share bad news or new ideas.

Crappy leaders are like that. And that's not you. You're a leader with a high emotional quotient—not a leader who lets their amygdala hijack them.

How Princess Elsa managed her 'Amygdala hijack' in Frozen

Princess Elsa understands leadership, and how to control her emotions. And how to control her ice-making superpower, especially when she gets out of control. Or at least now she does.

The movie Frozen (or the musical—which Mrs G and I went to see recently in Brisvegas) is an amazing lesson in leadership. Yes, we love musicals. And yes, we were among the only couples there without kids (i.e., the big kids).

For those of you with children, I'm guessing you'll be familiar with the plot. If you haven't seen the movie (which I haven't), the plot is about a princess who is to become queen. Princess Elsa can turn things, like hearts, to ice—if she doesn't control her emotions, that is. Because of that, Elsa is separated from other humans. Including her little sister Anna, who is shattered to lose contact with her big sis. A sad part of the story.

In psychology, the loss of emotional control is called an amygdala hijack. In short, being triggered causes an emotional reaction. That reaction causes us to 'fly off the handle' for want of a better description. We say and do things that are uncool. Then feel sorry, and maybe even say sorry, afterwards. When we've calmed down.

Overcoming an amygdala hijack is about responding, not reacting. Reacting is not the preferred option, as Princess Elsa finally worked out.

So, what can we learn about EQ from Princess Elsa?

ONE PRINCESS ELSA KNEW THAT SHE WAS RESPONSIBLE FOR HER IMPACT ON OTHERS.

Princess Elsa was very caring. She knew that her behaviour impacted on others, and that her amygdala hijacks could be dangerous. Very dangerous. As a leader, Elsa knew that she could have a serious long-term impact on others if she couldn't control her emotions.

Most leaders don't understand that you can heal or harm, help or hurt. Choose your language, and behaviour, to choose the former of each.

TWO PRINCESS ELSA KNEW SHE HAD AN ISSUE, AND SHE ADDRESSED IT.

Princess Elsa took an extreme action. She removed herself from other humans until she could be sure she could stay in control. She even got some gloves to cover her hands, to make sure no ice came out of them and froze people. In short, she did what it took to learn how to behave differently.

LEADER ACTION

Being in control is a learnt behaviour. If you give yourself permission to react, instead of responding appropriately, it might be time to think about new strategies for emotional control.

THREE PRINCESS ELSA NEVER STOPPED CARING.

Princess Elsa saved her little sister Anna, with 'an act of true love'. Elsa was able to undo the hurt she'd caused: she thawed Anna's heart. She never stopped caring and looking out for Anna (while the theatre was shedding a tear—a beautiful moment in the musical!).

LEADER ACTION

Leadership is about Extreme Ownership and taking responsibility for your 'emotional wake' (Credit Susan Scott[25] in Fierce Conversations). Keep caring and try to undo any hurt. ASAP.

Developing your EQ isn't a quick process, especially if you've been operating in amygdala hijack most of your life. But it's more than worth it, to become a transformational leader—and a stoic one.

HOW TO BE A STOIC LEADER

One of the words that I hear more and more often now is the word 'stoic'. And that people are trying to be more stoic. Or be like the stoics, the great stoic philosophers (Epictetus, Seneca, and Marcus Aurelius).

Marcus Aurelius is my favourite stoic philosopher, and he left us with some great quotes and some great ways to live and to lead.

Marcus Aurelius Antoninus (26 April 121 CE–17 March 180 CE) was Rome's emperor from 161 to 180 CE (and a Stoic philosopher). He was the last of the rulers known as the Five Good Emperors (a term coined some thirteen centuries later by Niccolò Machiavelli), and the last emperor of the Pax Romana, an age of relative peace and stability for the Roman Empire, lasting from 27 BCE to 180 CE. He also served as a Roman consul in 140, 145, and 161 (Credit: Wiki).

In his book on Stoicism, John Bowman[1] explains that Stoicism is a 2,300-year-old Greek and Roman philosophy that addresses human happiness. As examples, on escape Seneca wrote, 'whatever your destination, you will be followed by your failings'; on death, Marcus Aurelius advised to 'be content with your allocation of time'; and on suicide, Epictetus suggested to 'quit the game when it no longer pleases you, and depart.'

For me, the thing that gets me about Marcus Aurelius, and the stoic philosophers in general, is how well they articulated the trials, the tribulations, and the tumultuousness of their time in quotes and questions. And how relevant, real, and relatable those quotes and questions still are for our lives and our leadership in the 2020s.

Let's unpack three Marcus Aurelius quotes and see how they pertain to leadership in the 2020s and beyond. And remember, as you read these quotes, they were written in the 2nd Century CE! (And if this section piques your interest, Google more information on the great stoic philosophers and see what else you can apply.)

> **If you're distressed by anything external, the pain is not due to the thing itself, but to your estimate of it; and this you have the power to revoke at any moment.**

This is my favourite stoic quote. The quote talks to the fact that we have the power to choose our story, to choose our state, and to choose our strategy. The situation, event, or circumstance does not own us; we own how we respond to it, and we can choose to respond well.

In short, we can rephrase, reframe, and refocus any situation, to find a more positive or more pragmatic way to tell the story of what's happened. And things don't happen to us, they happen for us, so they can work through us.

Yes, leadership can be stressful, and it can be filled with challenges and curve balls. It can be filled with BOOM events that throw your day, month, or even your year off kilter. The great leaders realise that it's not the event that matters, but how we respond to it.

The same event will also have a different meaning for different people.

Which is the great thing about being human: we all have a different tale to tell (even of the same event).

The message is to be aware of how you're internalising things. You're in control, and it's not what happens to you, but how you respond, that matters. (Incidentally, I thought I came up with those words, but it's another famous stoic quote—go figure).

> **Every hour, focus your mind attentively on the performance of the task in hand, with dignity, human sympathy, benevolence, and freedom, and leave aside all other thoughts. You will achieve this if you perform each action as if it were your last.**

As a leader, are you interested, or are you totally committed? I mean, is leadership something that you show up for, or is it something that you show up with?

A lot of leaders have been promoted into the role. They've fallen into it. Or they've landed there. Because no one else was available at the time. That's showing up for leadership. For the pay cheque, or for the job title.

When you show up with leadership, you show up with a commitment to your team, your organisation, and your visions and values. You're showing up with the right intent, and with a clear why. You're showing up with a presence that communicates your commitment and your dedication to being the leader your team needs and deserves.

When you show up with leadership, you show up with presence and with congruence (your words match your actions). And you show up with attention to the task at hand. With the virtues of dignity, sympathy, benevolence, and freedom. And then, so does your team! The message is to be present, and to be focused on your tasks, and your team members (not at the same time).

> **In a sense, people are our proper occupation. Our job is to do them good and put up with them. But when they obstruct our proper tasks, they become irrelevant to us—like sun, wind, and animals. Our actions may be impeded by them, but there can be no impeding our intentions or our dispositions. Because we can accommodate and adapt. The mind adapts and converts to its own purposes the obstacle to our acting. The impediment to action advances action. What stands in the way becomes the way.**

This quote really resonates with me. I love it. Because my mission is to leave people better than I found them. While being firm when required, fair when required, and friendly when required. But always with a focus on feelings and factors that matter.

The second part of this quote talks about our intent, and our disposition. With the right intent, as I tell leaders everywhere, nothing can go wrong. You may offend, but you can apologise. You may upset, but you can reverse that. You may hurt, but you can heal that, with the right intent.

Intent is why you're doing something, whereas disposition is how you're doing it. If you can line both of these up in the right direction, watch your influence improve.

The message is to be very clear on your intent and know that humans are your key concern. At one end, leave people better than you found them. At the other end, at least aim for doing no harm. Help, not hurt. Heal not harm.

The great stoic quotes are quotes to live by. They contain so much wisdom that we can lean into now, and in the future, to develop our EQs and our ability to lead others purposefully and meaningfully.

As a footnote, my favourite Marcus Aurelius story is about how he tried to stay grounded. The story goes that Marcus Aurelius hired an assistant to follow him as he walked through the Roman towns square. The assistant's only role was to, whenever Marcus Aurelius was praised, whisper in his ear, 'You're just a man. You're just a man.' (Credit: Medium.com).

WHAT LEADERSHIP MEANS TO ME

I'm feeling reflective. I'm feeling like answering some big questions. For myself, as much as for my audience. This is part of developing EQ as a leader—unpacking what leadership means to you, and why.

I encourage you to do the same. As you read this section, be thinking about what leadership means to you, and how you came to believe those things about leadership and about teams.

For me, leadership is about influence, inspiration, and being impactful. Here's why.

ONE INFLUENCE.

For me, the key skill of leadership is the skill of influence. Being able to influence behaviour is crucial. Being able to influence thinking is also important, if you want to get people on board.

If I reflect on the best leaders that I've had, I feel like they were able to move my heart and mind in a direction that was towards what needed to be done. And towards understanding why things needed to be done.

My reflection here is that influence could be used for both good and for bad, but good leaders have the right intent, and that intent is to help their teams live into the values of the team and the values of the business. And that is at the heart of influence: helping team members mobilise their energy and to point it in the right direction—in the direction of the team's and organisation's values, goals, and objectives.

Influence starts with setting the direction. Then sharing it. Then influencing others to buy in.

To me, influence is about leadership languaging more than anything. Using words to engage and encourage others.

I think about great leaders on the planet, and I think about Barrack Obama, and how his speaking work was extremely engaging. And memorable. Obama was a leader who is remembered for his articulation and his charisma. Key elements of influence.

TWO INSPIRATION.

This is the biggie. The thing. The king. Inspiring others to follow you.

Inspiration is different to motivation. For me, motivation is very much an internal thing. It's generally something that people have or would like to have. 'I want to be more motivated,' you'll hear people saying. Inspiration is giving people something to work towards.

Because they can see you, as their leader, demonstrating the behaviour needed to deliver on not only what's required, but what's possible. Inspiration is about helping people understand their own potential, and then leaning into that potential because they can see you as their leader doing it.

Inspirational leadership is leading from the front. It's leading through action. It's leading from impossible to its possible. It's about demonstrating what could happen if your team follow your lead.

I think about great leaders on the planet, and I think about someone like Elon Musk, who can inspire massive workforces to accomplish massive goals and objectives. Even if those goals and objectives seem crazy at the start, Elon can inspire action.

THREE IMPACT.

My reflection is that leadership is the second most important job on planet Earth, behind parenting. Just think about being in the workforce for forty years of your life and having poor leaders for even some of that time.

Leaders are hugely important humans. And the sad part is that some of them don't know or believe that. A lot of leaders are in their roles because they were the next in line. Or because it pays more. Or because the manager was on leave. Not because they were right for it. And it's certainly not always because they really want to have an impact on other humans.

When I say impact, I mean being life changing. I mean being memorable, for the right reasons. I mean making a difference.

Having an impact means being present when needed. It means being purposeful with your intent. And it means being pumped about people. And understanding why they need to be your focus.

Fun fact: leaders that come through our leadership training programs can remember conversations with their leaders from decades ago. And they remember the crappy conversations more than the positive ones. They can remember the leaders that impacted them negatively.

To me, leadership is about having a positive impact on other humans.

I think about great leaders on the planet, and I think about Oprah Winfrey or Jacinda Ardern, who appear to care for others, and that comes through in their languaging and in their behaviour.

It's about influence, inspiration, and impact for me. Develop your EQ by thinking about what it means to you, and what you can learn about being an influential and transformative leader from other leaders.

WHAT CAN WE LEARN FROM OUR LEADERS?

One of my takes on leadership is that we don't spend enough time reflecting on the leaders we've had in the past (or present) and trying to learn from them. We've all had some outstanding leaders, and some not so great. But they can all teach us something about EQ, whether it's what to do more of, or what to do less of, to perform well in a leadership role.

There's a great stoic quote that says: 'As long as you live, keep learning how to live' (Credit: Seneca). In the 2020s, this quote could read: 'As long as you lead, keep learning how to lead.' One of the ways that we can keep learning is to reflect, recognise, and replace. Reflect on what good leaders do. Recognise what you would not do as a leader. Replace any strategies with new ones, and try new things.

Here are three questions to help you with this process.

ONE   WHAT HAVE MY FAVOURITE LEADERS DONE WELL? (THROUGH REFLECTION.)

This is a question that I ask at the start of our leadership programs. We fill the whiteboard with the best traits of our favourite leaders. We even use first names, to make it personal. Some of the time, mums and dads or grandparents make the list, which is beautiful, too.

In that half-hour session, we get such a great vibe going, and we reflect on why our favourite leaders had such an impact on us, and how they did that. Then more specifically, how we felt and how we responded to those leaders. Integrity always comes up, as do a range of other positive values and behaviour-based adjectives. That session is such a positive way to start two days of training.

That exercise is designed to provide an overview of the traits of the best leaders we have all experienced. At times, it's a sports star, or a movie star, whose name is mentioned; but at the end of that discussion, we have a list of traits that we can lean into. And maybe one day when we do that exercise, your name will make the list, because of how you lead others.

LEADER ACTION

Spend a moment or two, now, reflecting on the best leaders you've experienced, and what made them so outstanding. Also consider what you could do differently.

TWO   WHAT HAVE MY FAVOURITE LEADERS DONE POORLY? (THROUGH RECOGNITION.)

Would you believe that we used to ask this question at the start of our leadership programs (before I changed it to the one above)? I changed it up when I recognised what a negative spin it put on the program and on the workshop, which was hard to come back from.

Yes, everyone has a story of a poor leader. Yes, some of these stories are decades old. And yes, this is what not to do, and the message is that if you want to be a good leader, don't do these things. But it still put the attendees in a negative emotional state.

And that's what happens when we experience poor leadership. Instead of just saying that we feel crappy, or hurt, or not valued, we need to recognise what the behaviour was that made us feel that way, so that we can make sure we don't repeat it in our own leadership.

Specifically, recognise what it was that the leader did when they had the worst impact on your emotional state. It's generally because they were under pressure, they had no people skills, or they were only worried about themselves and not the team (or some variation of these three).

LEADER ACTION

Spend a moment or two, now, reflecting on the worst leaders you've experienced, and what made them so memorable. Recognise what you'd never do as a leader, based on these experiences.

THREE WHAT WOULD (INSERT NAME HERE) DO IN THIS SITUATION? (THROUGH REPLACEMENT.)

Whether it's your favourite leader, someone you aspire to be like, or even your leadership coach, pick someone that does well in the tough situations that you might encounter, whether it's leading under pressure or building rapport with people skills. Then, when you're faced with the same difficult situation, ask yourself the question: what would that person do now?

This is one of the best tools I've learnt over time. I have names like Tony Robbins for my speaking work. Or Richard Branson as a leader. And of course, people closer to home and people I know well. With this question, I find I can replace limiting beliefs and limiting behaviours very quickly. It helps me take a new approach to the situation I'm facing. It makes me think differently, and think about what someone else would do in this situation— someone who's getting better results that I am in that area!

LEADER ACTION

Spend a moment or two, now, thinking about what types of thinking or behaviour you might like to replace in order to get a better result in a specific area of your life or leadership.

When you reflect on what leaders have done well or poorly, you'll be able to see the corresponding EQ involved. It's a good way to develop your own, and to identify maladaptive emotional responses that you can steer away from or replace with effective ones. It's a long-term commitment, but well worth the effort to become a good leader—as good a leader as the ones you admire the most—even when you're under pressure.

THE STRESS VERSUS DURESS QUANDARY

So, you're feeling under pressure right now. My coaching clients are talking about the COVID-19 'crisis' that they're dealing with. Including how do they keep their workplaces safe? How do they ask for proof of vaccinations, and the myriad of things that come with a pandemic? Things we haven't seen before, and hopefully won't again.

With the crisis comes the requirement to stay in control, to have care factor for their teams, and be courageous enough to make the tough decisions that need to be made. It all feels like more pressure. But is the pressure a form of stress, or is it a type of duress? And does it matter?

IS IT STRESS?

The Merriam-Webster dictionary shares that the phrase 'under duress' should not be confused with 'under stress'. Stress is concerned with strain or pressure, while duress refers to wrongful or unlawful coercion.

Stress is very much an internal response. It's an emotional reaction. It's akin to anxiety or panic, and it affects different people differently. But it's very much the bodily reaction to either external or internal stimuli, which might come from applied duress, from worrying about the economy, from worrying about your team, or from having to write a COVID-19 response plan when you have no idea where to start. That's stress. That's you sitting at your desk staring at your blank screen, trying to unpack what they heck is going on around you, and why you can't think clearly, and why you can't find a way to get into action.

Prolonged, or chronic, stress leads to a wide range of mental and physical and complications, including death. Ask anyone in Japan about Karoshi (working themselves to death). That's the perfect example of how you can put enough stress on your body that eventually it will shut down. Maybe even at your desk.

Typically, when you're stressed, you'll be berating yourself for not getting something in on time, or pushing yourself to meet the deadline, or cursing yourself for not being able to do a specific task and being worried about asking for help. Or it might be the fear that you experience when you need to do a public speech.

LEADER ACTION

If you're feeling stressed, there are techniques that you can lean into to help you clear your mind and clear your emotional slate. They include breathing, affirmations, meditation, and mindfulness (BAMM).

IS IT DURESS?

Duress is a totally different kettle of fish (a very technical-ish idiom for a muddle). The reason that duress is such a muddle is that it's externally applied. It's applied by another human. Generally, your leader. Yes, duress is a big deal, because it is, as defined above, a form of coercion. The politically correct leader who is applying duress would call it persuasion; the person under duress would call it manipulation at best, threatening at worst. Basically, duress is bad. Really bad.

Duress (in my mind) is just another word for 'poor leadership' and 'not being able to lead under pressure.' Herein lies the most important point of this section, as it talks straight to one of the first reactions that leaders have when they're under stress. The s@#$ flows downhill, right? If I'm stressed, I need to make it yours (my team members). Then I'll feel better. And they won't. Uncool. But I still hear it.

The duress might not just come from a leader who's stressed. It can come from a leader at any time, when they don't realise, like Spiderman, that leadership comes with great responsibility. Harvard Business Review explains that leaders can stress out (or duress) their team members, even unintentionally,[7] by using negative language, through erratic actions, emotional volatility, excessive pessimism, or by ignoring people's emotions. It's really uncool working for a leader like that. Especially over the long term or over a prolonged period.

A 2003 study[16] by Charlie Marsh proposed that posttraumatic stress disorder (PTSD) and so-called 'prolonged duress stress disorder' (PDSD) have similar symptom profiles, and differ only with regard to the presence or absence of a 'traumatic event.' What this study found was that enough duress-enforced stress can have the same impact on a human as a traumatic event. That is big.

LEADER ACTION

If you're a leader and you're reflecting on the above stressors that you may inflict on your team, never fear: there is an answer. The answer is learning how to lead under pressure (LUP). Take steps to build your LUP skills, and take ownership of your emotional state, your own stress levels, and how you treat others when you're stressed.

DOES IT MATTER?

If you're struggling with pressure, yes, it does matter if it's stress or duress, because there are two very different action plans depending on what you're experiencing. For stress, it's about emotional control. For duress, it's a robust conversation with the person applying the duress, in relation to how you're feeling and how it's affecting you (simple to say, not as easy to do). A hard conversation, but an important one.

For leaders who are constantly in fight-or-flight mode, or who feel like the COVID-19 crisis is getting the better of you, my coaching would include to stay in emotional control (whatever that takes), have care factor for your team (they are struggling too) and be courageous in your decision making (ensuring the decisions are legal, moral and ethical, of course). Email me to unpack your Leadership Resilience Review (a 15-minute diagnostic that will talk you through pressure relief opportunities).

Let's close this chapter out with why, as a leader, having sufficient EQ to manage your stress and not apply duress is important to your team. One of the best research papers I've read on the topic of employee job satisfaction was produced by Prakash Singh in 2013. The study unpacked the importance of emotional intelligence (and emotional control) for leaders, explaining that employees prefer to be led by leaders who are confident in their leadership role, who send out clear, unambiguous messages, who maintain self-control, who are adaptable and flexible, who face the future with optimism, and who help build a collegial working environment.

Just imagine for a moment if we, as leaders, used all of those skills, and imagine how satisfied and productive our teams would be.

ACTIVITY 2.3
DEVELOP YOUR EMOTIONAL QUOTIENT

Take some time now to think about what you've learnt in the last chapter.

The series of questions on the following pages will encourage you to think about what you can do to develop your emotional quotient, and how you can apply the lessons you've just learnt in upskilling your leadership.

Otherwise, think about how manage your emotions in the workplace, and ways you could upskill your leadership with improved emotional consistency and better resilience.

What could you work on so your communication is more holistic?

What activities could you engage in to create better emotional control?

What impact has your emotional intelligence, or lack of it, had on your team members or employees?

What does leadership mean to you? Influence? Inspiration? Impact? Or something else?

Think about some of your past leaders. What did they do well, or not so well?

Imagine a favourite leader dealing with a leadership issue you're dealing with right now. What would they do?

Can you think of constructive ways to manage your stress?

Answer honestly. Do you think your team members or employees experience duress, either from you, or another leader?

SKILL IV

LEAD UNDER PRESSURE

WHEN WE LOOK AT SOME LEADERS, WE KNOW THAT THEY DON'T HAVE SELF-CONTROL, AND THEY DON'T HAVE CREDIBILITY.

Their catch line is to 'do as I say, not as I do' and you never quite know if they're really going to follow through on what they said they'll do.

Don't be like those leaders.

Why? Because those leaders can't be trusted to follow through, to follow processes, or to follow their own mandate of putting people first. And not only can't we trust them. They can't trust themselves. But what does it mean to have self-trust, when you're leading under pressure?

No discussion on trust will be complete without a reference to Stephen M. R. Covey,[ ] who authored the book The Speed of Trust. In that book, the first and most critical element of trust is self-trust. Following through on the commitments you make, firstly to yourself, and then to your team.

Let me explain.

ONE SELF-TRUST IS ABOUT COMMITMENT.

To be the leader that you know you can be is about making personal and life commitments and sticking to those commitments. For example, get the simple things sorted. Get up with the alarm, or before it, not snooze it five times. Go to the gym on the days you say you will. Set goals, and work towards them. Read the book that you committed to reading.

Some of these might feel or seem like simple things, but they're not. They're confidence builders. If you increase your self-confidence, you'll make better decisions. You'll feel better about yourself, and your ability to follow through outside of work. Keeping your commitments to yourself is a big deal.

TWO SELF-TRUST IS ABOUT CREDIBILITY.

To be a leader that people want to follow, you need to be credible. Aka: being believable. Convincing. Persuasive. To be credible, leaders need to have the two core attributes: competence and character. Competence to know what's happening in their team, and why. And character, to have the courage to make the calls that need to be made, with integrity, with the right intent, and with the right delivery.

Sometimes the right decisions are not the easiest or the most straight forward. But they're the decisions that are the most legal, moral, and ethical. When you're operating in the legal, moral, and ethical space, your team will see how you demonstrate character (and courage). And you'll trust yourself to do what's right, not what's easy.

THREE SELF-TRUST IS ABOUT CONSISTENCY.

Consistency of emotional state, consistency of response (not reaction), and consistency of behaviour. This is about self-awareness as much as self-trust. Knowing how your physical and emotional state changes under pressure and being prepared to advance through adversity when the challenge or the pressure arrives is about being self-aware and consistent.

And of course, there's no time when self-trust is more important than when you're under stress or pressure. Leadership under pressure requires trusting yourself to be in conscious control, and operating with care factor, to make the tough decisions.

Sometimes, off the bat, and in public.

THE CHRIS ROCK REACTION WAS A LESSON IN SELF-CONTROL

Recently I got asked by a leader to unpack the saga that was played out between Chris Rock and Will Smith at the Oscars. (Which will go down in history as the slapping event that occurred following a Chris Rock joke that wasn't part of the script.)

It was obviously too personal, and not well thought through, in the moment.

So, here's my take on what it means for leading under pressure (noting that my take won't be what you expect. And won't be as direct as the opinions of people like Jim Carrey, who publicly asked for an assault charge to be laid).

Will Smith first though, only briefly, even though it was his action that we're really talking about. In his apology on Twitter the following day (which appeared to be sincere, and heartfelt), Smith used the words: 'I reacted emotionally.' Yes, he did. He gave himself permission in the moment to not process information, and not to respond, but to react.

But the big picture first.

ONE WHAT'S THE REAL CULTURE OF THE OSCARS?

'Where are you going with this one?', you might think. Well, what I go straight to when it comes to episodes like this is what was it about the culture that contributed to it? There's a thought. What encouraged it?

There's been a lot of commentary about the fact that (paraphrasing here) the presenters are going to make jokes from the stage, and the actors need to suck it up. Seriously, the stars presenting the awards would have had months to come up with material to use on stage. Surely we don't have to make it normal to make jokes about people? Surely Chris Rock (who I love, BTW, as I do Will Smith) can do better than that. He's a funny human. He doesn't need to take the mickey out of people.

Or is it just me that feels that you can be funny without being insulting? Why risk hurting other humans when you don't need to, just to be funny? Help me out—what am I missing here?

FYI, there have been actors come out and say that what occurred on stage after a personal joke was their greatest fear. It kept them up at night. Here's a thought—change the joke. You might even get more sleep.

The excuse will be that Chris Rock didn't know about the health condition of Jada Pinkett Smith. Not good enough, in my view. I hope the Oscars read my post on the subject, and address this.

TWO CHRIS ROCK'S RESPONSE WAS NEAR PERFECT.

'Will Smith just smacked the shit out of me,' Chris Rock said, while Smith walked off stage after slapping him. 'Wow, dude,' Rock continued, 'It was a G.I. Jane joke.'

Watch the video closely, and you'll see Chris Rock respond (NOT react) to being publicly slapped. Most viewers (I guess) would have expected him to respond like that.

But here's the alternative. Imagine this: Chris Rock hits back. There's a fight on stage. They roll off the stage together wrestling. Other actors have to rush in to stop the melee. It can't be stopped, and security are called, and on it goes. I believe that could have happened.

The poise and presence that Chris Rock displayed in the immediate moments after the incident says so much about his emotional intelligence and emotional control. His facial expression was disbelief first, then questioning—what just happened? He was processing. Deciding how to respond. Putting the incident through his frontal lobes, not through his limbic system (the emotional brain). You can nearly see his brain working through his body language (which was actually very open, and not aggressive in any way).

Chris Rock saved the night. Saved the event. And I hope he gets credit for that, instead of just the internet bashing of Will Smith. That self-control is a key skill in leading under pressure, equal in importance to empathy.

THE KEY SKILL FOR LEADING UNDER PRESSURE

The key skill for leading under pressure is empathy. And for those who've heard that before, read on, because not a lot of people really understand what empathy is.

In a blog post (What Empathy Really Takes), I unpacked the fact that empathy takes action, and it's neither an emotion nor an automatic reaction. It's not sympathy, and it's not just about trying to understand what someone is going through.

Empathy is about action (that is the compassion piece: there is no compassion without action). Empathy starts with a cognitive understanding of what someone is going through, then having an emotional connection to their struggle, and finally doing something (where possible) to support them—although this is not always possible. This methodology was developed by Daniel Goleman,[ii] and it provides a great framework for what empathy is and how to put it into practice. Which is what leaders need to do when they're under pressure. And the pressure might be to deal with a team member who's struggling.

It's in these moments that empathy is critical. Brene Brown defined empathy as 'holding the space'. Being present when someone is sharing their toughest times with you.

In our leadership programs, we train the topic of empathy. And the best way to train it is to use a story from a coaching client who applied it beautifully.

Our client (the leader) was struggling with the absenteeism of a team member. We put a plan together to have the discussion, with empathy being at the heart of the conversation. We suspected that there was an issue outside of work, and it turned out there was. And it was a deeply personal issue that the team member shared, one that the leader had never experienced. The concern for the team member (whose performance had also dropped due to the challenges they were facing), translated into more time off to deal with it.

The leader put themselves in the shoes of the team member, and could then think and feel what it would be like for the team member. Once the leader understood both the issue, and how to support their team member, it was time to actually support the team member. Following the conversation, the leader consulted the HR team (the action piece: compassion), and it turned out that there was a specific type of leave to cover just such a situation. The leader was able to help the team member to get the time off that they needed to deal with the issue; the team member was then able to work through it, and to come back to work with a better mindset. The team member was also grateful for the support.

The key thing in this case study is the leader taking action. The understanding is the first part of empathy, but the compassion is the most important part. While leaders can't always take action like this to support their team members during these periods, they should certainly try.

Some tips to help leaders to be more empathetic include:

- Asking great questions to learn more about the person and their lives
- Then, listening to understand, not to respond
- Being attentive to body language and other types of nonverbal communication (behaviour includes emotions)
- Not necessarily agreeing, but understanding the situation and the position of the other person
- Putting yourself in the other person's shoes

And the most important thing: going out of your way to do something that supports your team member. Yes, I know you're busy, and you've got so much to do, and people take up so much time, and it's like 90% of your job, and you don't get time to yourself (all said with love—I just hear this a lot).

We're all born compassionate. I got asked at a recent program 'well, if we're all born compassionate, why don't some leaders act like that?' I'll leave you with that one.

You can't lead well under pressure without empathy, compassion, and self-control. All of those elements are about the people you're leading and responding to. But what about what you need, as a leader, to be able to keep on track in your leadership journey, when you're putting out fires every day? That's where resilience comes in.

HOW TO BE RESILIENT WHEN LEADING UNDER PRESSURE

Resilience is not just about coping. Resilience is about being ready to cope when you need to. There is a great definition of resilience, from @JurieRossow, who defines it as 'advancing despite adversity'.

I love this take.

So, if resilience is about both preparing for a BOOM event, and then advancing through it, what are the skills required at each end of the process? And how do you learn them?

For me, and from my lived experience, resilience is about turning life's lessons into life's blessings. And working out what you could take from the BOOM event that would set you up for success into the future—aka, if the same thing happened again, how would you deal with it a second time, or even a third time? And deal with it better?

In short, we go from living to learning, through a five-stage process that starts with living a life of blessing, living through the BOOM event, to living a life of learning. And the quicker we can get to the learning stage after the event, the sooner we stop ruminating (or thinking negatively) about what happened and what else we should have done.

Let's unpack what you can do before and after the BOOM event, to help you advance despite adversity.

ONE UNDERSTAND YOUR PR6.

As a certified Resilience Coach (though Hello Driven), I've been able to learn about both the neurological and the behavioural elements of resilience building. From a skill set perspective, your Personal Resilience 6 are the six life skills that will help you to be prepared for a BOOM event. They include:

- **Vision:** Having meaning, purpose, congruence, and goals for your life
- **Composure:** Being calm and in control, with emotional regulation, self-awareness, and stress management
- **Reasoning:** Adaptability, problem solving, resourcefulness, anticipation, and planning
- **Health:** Getting quality sleep, eating well, and exercising regularly
- **Tenacity:** Being persistent, bouncing back, being realistically

optimistic, and staying motivated

- **Collaboration:** Through strong relationships, support networks, and teamwork

Note that we can send you a link through Hello Driven **to complete your resilience profile, and learn ways to improve your resilience.** The more you understand the PR6, you better prepared you'll be for any BOOM event.

TWO LEARN THE SKILL OF REFRAMING.

Of the PR6 skills that you can develop, prior to a BOOM event, the one that you'll rely on following a BOOM is the skill of reframing. Or rephrasing. Or reprogramming.

For me personally, the ability to reframe is the best and most useful life skill I've learnt in all my years on planet Earth. By far. This is not the first time that I've said that, and it won't be the last. But what is reframing?

Glad you asked. Reframing is quite a simple skill (simple, but not easy at times), that helps you put a positive spin on any situation or event. It's like finding the silver lining in the dark cloud. It's about focusing on what went right, not what went wrong, and it's about learning from the BOOM event, so that when you talk about it, you talk about it in a positive sense.

You talk about it from a philosopher perspective, not a victim perspective. And you get to the point where you can even share those learnings with others, so that they might be better prepared if they were ever to encounter a similar situation.

Reframing is as much about rephrasing as anything else: about the language that you use, both with your inside voice, and with your outside voice. If you check yourself, you'll notice that you're using either negative words to explain the event, or you're more positive about it. When you get to that stage, you'll know that reframing work is paying off, and that you're starting to look at the event with a different perspective—which, in turn, will help you to stop ruminating about it. Winner!

As a side note, people that have been through traumatic BOOM events, and can take the lessons from the event, have been said to demonstrate PTG (post traumatic growth). And of course, there are people who struggle to get through those events, and sadly the result can be PTSD.

THREE KNOW THAT COPING IS A NECESSARY PART OF LIFE.

Yes, there will be times that you'll have to cope. You'll have to suffer through some tough times. If you haven't yet, go you, congrats. But they are coming. One in two people in Australia will suffer through a mental health challenge sometime in their lives.

Coping is a crucial skill. The more resilient you are, the easier it will be to cope with whatever life throws at you. That's never more true when you're leading under pressure, and the wellbeing of all the people in your team, organisation, and its market are depending on you.

Always look for ways to improve your resilience. One of the best ways I've found is through the practice of gratitude.

BEING GRATEFUL IS PART OF BUILDING YOUR RESILIENCE

There are people on the planet that would love your life. They'd love the freedom that you have, the health that you have, the relationship that you have, and even the struggles that you have. There are people on the planet that would be grateful to be in your position.

And I will, for the sake of this section, presume that you're happy to be in the position you're in, too. But I will also presume, that like most people, you don't spend too much time thinking about how grateful you are, and even less time physically writing down or journalling about the things or people you're grateful for.

The wellbeing benefits of being grateful have been well studied, researched, and documented. And like all good theories, gratitude is not new: it's been espoused by some of the great philosophers, going back as far as the second century. One Marcus Aurelius quote says that 'All you need are these: certainty of judgment in the present moment; action for the common good in the present moment; and an attitude of gratitude in the present moment for anything that comes your way.' So, if gratitude can help the last of the great rulers known as the Five Good Roman Emperors, maybe it can work for us too.

But like everything in our lives that makes a difference, it takes work, and it takes effort. The effort is worth it, though, as gratitude is linked to increased levels of happiness, resilience, and relationships. That means you benefit, and so do the people you're leading.

If you're looking for things to be grateful for, here's a few.

ONE GRATITUDE FOR HAPPINESS & OTHER POSITIVE EMOTIONS.

Sheldon and Lyubomirsky (2006) studied whether or not gratitude could have an impact on our emotional state. Sonja Lyubomirsky[26] herself appears to study happiness more than gratitude. But in an attempt to understand what can change our mood (and make us happy), her work inevitably led to gratitude. Lyubomirsky called it 'counting our blessings.' The study reported that expressing gratitude (being thankful and appreciative) elevates our positive emotions. Why? Because it 'fosters the savouring of positive life experiences and situations, so that people can extract the maximum possible satisfaction and enjoyment from their circumstances.' Gratitude prevents people from taking good things for granted. The expression of gratitude is thought to also increase stimulate moral behaviour (like paying it forward), which in turn also increases happiness. Being happy, and feeling good about ourselves, and about our situation, helps us to enjoy life more.

The caveat, though, is that it only has that effect if we practice gratitude on a regular basis, preferably daily.

TWO GRATITUDE FOR RESILIENCE.

In his groundbreaking and 'unputdownable' book, The Resilience Project, Hugh van Cuylenburg talked through the GEM process, which is gratitude, empathy, and mindfulness. In that book, van Cuylenburg unpacked the power of gratitude and the amazing benefits it brings in relation to how resilient we are in our everyday lives. Feeling grateful changes our brain chemistry in a way that makes rumination more difficult.

Rumination is 'getting stuck' and not being able to get past a situation or a conversation or an event that troubled you or that you didn't handle well in the moment. Rumination can be debilitating it not addressed with improved self-talk (and even Cognitive Behavioural Therapy, or CBT). Gratitude helps you to stop ruminating, to cope with what has happened, and move through it to 'advance through adversity' (the definition of resilience). In short, gratitude increases your resilience by reducing your rumination, and helping you to bounce back quicker. Who wouldn't love to be a able to do that?

THREE GRATITUDE FOR RELATIONSHIPS.

Just imagine for a moment all of the amazing humans that you've been fortunate enough to be exposed to during your life, and how many of them have helped shape you into the great human you are today. So, how grateful as you for all of their support? And would you be the human you are without all of their input, guidance, coaching, support, nurturing and care? Possibly not (and, yes, for anyone reading this that is thinking about all of the people that have wronged you—believe it or not, they've helped you too, by helping you learn a lesson in life).

The message is that our relationships shape our life. The great business philosopher (aka motivational speaker) Tony Robbins[20] famously states that 'the quality of your life is in direct proportion to the quality of your relationships.' And this is so true. Higher-quality relationships equate to a higher-quality life. And then there's the find-remind-and-bind theory. The theory posits that the positive emotion of gratitude serves the evolutionary function of strengthening a relationship with a responsive interaction partner (Algoe, Haidt, & Gable, 2008).[2] In short, the more grateful we are, the better we are at connecting with others, and building relationships through interactions and conversation. Remember that we are both a primitive species living a modern existence, as well as a social creature craving connecting. Being grateful helps us connect.

BUT HOW DO I START?

Being grateful is a very easy process. Take a minute now to think about what you're grateful for. Preferably, write it down: writing connects thoughts to the world around us, and once written, it can never be unwritten.

Just give thanks. Say aloud thank you for what ever it is you're thankful for. If you want to start practicing gratitude, please email me for a free electronic copy of your NOW Gratitude Journal, that you can use to get started.

Once you're in a gratitude mindset, it's easier to do the thinking work. Keep your eyes open, and you can learn from all kinds of people who are good under pressure—including triathletes, like yours truly.

WHAT LEADERS CAN LEARN FROM IRON WAR

An Ironman triathlon is arguably the toughest one-day endurance event on planet Earth. Ironman started in 1979, with three athletes arguing (over a beer, of course) about who the fittest athlete was. The 3.8 km swimmer. The 180 km cyclist. Or the 42.2 km runner.

There was only one solution. To put all three together and do them at the same time. And since that first event in 1979, the sport has become an institution for triathletes everywhere, with the pinnacle being the Hawaii Ironman World Championships, held every October in Kona.

The 1989 Ironman World Championship was perhaps the greatest Ironman race ever. In a spectacular duel that became known as the Iron War, the world's two strongest athletes raced side by side at world-record pace for a gruelling 139 miles.

Mark Allen, the calm, controlled, and composed athlete, was trying to win his first Ironman World Championship. Allen used technology, like heart rate monitoring and specific training programs. Dave Scott was the opposite. He was hardcore. His philosophy was to go out and bust yourself up, every session. No science.

Allen had never beaten Scott in Hawaii. Some people thought he never would. Allen finished second in 1986 and 1987, behind Scott.

So, Allen came up with a strategy. His plan was to race on Scott's shoulder for the whole race. For the whole eight hours. Mark Allen and Dave Scott raced shoulder to shoulder through Ironman's 3.8 km swim, 180 km bike race, and 42.2 km marathon. After eight punishing hours, both men would demolish the previous record—and cross the finish line a mere 58 seconds apart (See Matt Fitzgerald's[10] book, Iron War if you love this sport, or you just love the human species). The strategy worked.

Mark Allen won that race, to grab his first world title. He won it with a burst of energy, through an aid station in the final stages of the race.

What can we learn, as leaders, from this commitment to a cause?

ONE CHANGE THE STRATEGY, NOT THE GOAL.

For Mark Allen, he needed a strategy that worked. He and Scott had raced each other plenty of times, with Allen always coming in after Scott.

The goal to win the world championship never changed. The strategy changed. Until it worked, and the goal was achieved. Never change the goal—adapt the strategy.

For leaders, and for leadership teams, this is an important point, as there will be hurdles. There will be obstacles. There will be challenges. That doesn't mean you give up on your goal. It means that you're building resilience along the way. And that you're getting closer with every attempt.

TWO TUNE OUT THE NOISE.

There will be detractors. There will be dissenters. There will be disapproval.

But if your why is strong enough, you'll be able to tune out these voices, even when some of them are your own. As a leader or leadership team, you will be exposed to negativity. Noise. Nonsense.

Set yourself up for success and have a positive mindset. One that doesn't get distracted. For Mark Allen, there was a single-minded focus that drove his behaviour, and that got him to the finish line first during the Iron War.

Imagine for a moment how many people would have thought that, after he tried so many times previously that it seemed implausible that he would ever beat Dave Scott.

But Allen didn't listen to that noise. He didn't listen to the noise that would have distracted him from the mission.

THREE RINSE, REPEAT, AND REPRODUCE.

Fun fact: Mark Allen won that event in 1989, then again in 1990, then again in 1991, then again in 1992, and then again in 1993. Before 1989, Allen couldn't beat Scott. He then won five world championships in a row. He certainly rinsed, repeated, and reproduced what worked.

In relation to rinsing and repeating, the message is to find out what works, and do more of that. And find out what doesn't, and do less of that. Once you have the winning formula for your team, or your business, leverage it. Build on it and ingrain it in your organisational culture. So that you keep getting great results. Like Mark Allen did.

This section has focused on Mark Allen's strategy during Iron War, and what we can learn from that. But it wouldn't be right not to congratulate Dave Scott, too, who's one of the greatest athletes to ever do Ironman racing. Scott is a six-time world champion. A legend of the sport. And I was lucky enough to meet him at a race in Sydney some years ago. Fun fact again: an amazing Aussie Greg Welch won the event in 1994! Go Welchy!

Learn how to lead under pressure from people with grit. They never give up on a goal. They change the strategy, and keep cranking until they find the magic sauce. To do that, they tune out the noise. And once they've worked out the strategy for success, they rinse and repeat, and can reproduce the results they're committed to achieving.

You can do it, too. Here's some more pearls of leadership wisdom from the sport, about the endurance you need to upskill your leadership.

WHY DOING A TRIATHLON IS LIKE LEADING UNDER PRESSURE

Learning how to do something hard is worth the effort. Like a triathlon, and more specifically an endurance triathlon. A sporting event that takes between five and seventeen hours to complete, depending on how much training you've done. But even the short triathlons will be tough, especially when you're first starting out. A little bit like leadership.

And for anyone that doesn't know, a triathlon is a swim, ride, run event, where the bike leg is generally the longest leg of the event, compared to the swim and run. I've been doing triathlons since 2008, and I've learnt a lot about the sport, about myself, and about leadership during that time. Here's how triathlon and leading under pressure are similar, and how we can take lessons from one for the other.

No matter how many times you've lined up on the start line, the swim leg is a challenge. There is never a time in my life when I am surrounded by more people, but feel so alone. We're shoulder to shoulder on this line. Emotions are high, and energy levels are higher. I know that I'm about to be in the water, I'll be struggling for breath, and getting kicked and bumped (the swim is a contact sport) by other swimmers.

For the vast majority of first timers, or even experienced triathletes, the swim leg is not their strongest, so it takes courage and effort to 'toe the water' and to just dive straight in, when the buzzer goes off.

IT FEELS LIKE IT GOES ON FOREVER.

Jump into the challenge, catch your breath, take the bumps, and keep moving forward toward the buoys (goals).

Then it's time to jump on your bike and go for a little ride. The ride leg is good for thinking time and collecting yourself. I make sure I get my heart rate down, get into a rhythm, and focus on hydration and nutrition. The biggest challenge on the bike is overcooking it and going too hard. Remember, you still have a run to do at the end of the bike leg. Most triathletes have had the experience of pushing too hard on the bike and burning their legs for the run.

And of course, follow all the rules on the bike. Don't draft, don't litter, and don't obstruct other riders. Even when there are no technical officials watching. This is the big thing for the fast bikers. They like riding behind other fast bikers. Which is uncool.

AND THERE'S STILL MORE TO GO.

Remember that you have a long day ahead. Don't go too quickly too early, and always do the right thing, even when no one is watching (that's integrity).

Now it's time to run home. The age-old issue for triathletes who get off the bike: they hope their legs still work, and that they can control them. I've felt the jelly-leg effect on numerous occasions, and it's not pleasant. You want your legs to work, but they don't. It's a matter of getting composed and knowing that the feeling will come back soon.

But you get through that weird feeling and run (or walk) whatever distance is required. Until you cross that finish line and get the finish line feeling, that's like nothing else on planet Earth (big statement). I've completed a range of triathlon distances and have run a marathon at the end of a 180 km ride. Which was tough. Regardless of the distance, most triathletes manage to find some energy to finish strong.

AND IT HURTS THE WHOLE TIME, BUT IT'S A GOOD HURT.

Remain composed, know that you're getting closer to your goals (even if you're wobbly right now). And the most important part of leadership: celebrate success when you achieve what you set out to do.

Learn more about the sport of triathlon—it's a great way to learn about the journey of leadership, especially when you're leading under pressure.

ACTIVITY 2.4
LEAD UNDER PRESSURE

Answering the following questions will encourage you to think about what you can do to develop your ability to stay in control under pressure—and to strength yourself as a caring and impactful leader for your team. Alternatively, spend some time journalling about what you're grateful for, and how you could be more resilient.

Do you think your team members or employees see you as credible, and as having good character? Why, or why not?

In what ways could you support a team member who's struggling in their professional life? What about in their personal life?

Are you resilient when leading under pressure? Why, or why not?

Answer honestly. Do you follow through with your commitments? If not, how could you do this better?

How could you work on your emotional control so that you can 'tune out the noise' when you're under pressure?

SKILL V
BE COURAGEOUS

COURAGE: THE ABILITY TO ACT WHEN YOU DON'T WANT TO.

Courage. Without it, fear will stop you from ever moving forward with purpose. Full stop.

If there's one thing we know about leadership, it's that it takes a huge amount of courage. Courage to get started. Courage to keep moving. If you asked the great stoic philosopher, Seneca the Younger, he would have told you that 'sometimes, even to live is an act of courage'. And he's right. Living takes courage, and so does leadership.

Courage is about action. The right action. Even when you're scared. Even when you might not have all the information. But when you know something is the right thing to do.

This section isn't one of those motivational ones where I share with you the story of some great adventurer who was scared, but who got over the fear, and slayed the dragon and saved the fair maiden. (Wasn't Shrek a great movie?)

This section is specifically about when leaders need to display courage, and how they can do that. It's about courageous leadership, and the buckets of courage that it takes to be a courageous leader (Credit: wework.com)

ONE TRY COURAGE.

Fun fact. You might fail. You might fall. You might falter. But without the courage to try, you'll never even get started. You won't try new things. In his book The Courage to Start, John Bingham[1] talks about going from an overweight couch potato to running marathons, and how he would never have completed all of those runs if he didn't have the courage to start.

If you ask Will Smith, he'll say fail often and fail forward. I'm a big fan of those words, and I can say hand on heart, most of the things I've ever tried in business haven't worked. But they were lessons, in the end, not failures.

Here's the process. Have an idea. Tell the team. Get buy in (hopefully). Get started. You've got this—it just takes some try courage.

TWO TRUST COURAGE.

In my many years as a leadership coach, one of the things that I've heard the most is that 'if you need it done properly, you need to do it yourself.' Oh no, I think, this'll be a hard mindset to change. But it can be changed. If the leader is willing to give up control.

And if the leader is willing to see the qualities and the value that their team possesses. The infinite ability of the collective. Their power to be autonomous and to do their jobs better than their leader can. That's called transformational leadership, which is the leader having trust courage, and the team members having try courage. Winner.

Without trust, leaders will never create more leaders. They'll just create more work for themselves. And arrive at our next session being too busy.

You've got this—it just takes some trust courage.

THREE TELL COURAGE.

Tell them. In a way that's based on your conviction, your commitment, and your care factor. The better you can articulate your vision, the better your team can buy in and get working towards it.

Recently, we ran a two-day leadership workshop for leaders who want to make a difference, are willing to do what it takes, and are willing to stand up for something. That's the key. Part of that program will be for the leaders to unpack the first question of why they do leadership. The vast majority of our trainees have never thought about that question—why do I do what I do? It's the first thing that a leader should be able to tell others. And then, they can articulate it and tell it to engage people in the goals and objectives of the business or team. Winner.

You've got this—it just takes some tell courage.

LEADERS, HOW COURAGEOUS ARE YOU?

Courageous leaders can create a culture of trust and respect, which makes those around them be prepared to follow them. This all creates a recipe for success, development, and evolution within an organisation.

As a young leader, I was scared (petrified, really) of things like making big decisions. Having robust discussions. Trusting others to do important work. And the advice I got was quite broad: just get over your fears. Act in spite of fear. Courage is not the absence of fear; it's acting anyway.

All great ideas (and cliches), and I get them. For sure. But what do they really mean?

Do they mean 'stop procrastinating'? Do they mean 'you're afraid of public speaking; join Toastmasters'? Do they mean 'stop overthinking it and get into action'? I feel like those quotes are quite broad, even for a broad topic like courage. I feel that leaders need better advice, they need better guidance, and they need clearer actions. Why? Because leadership is not broad, it's one discussion, one conversation at a time.

Courageous leaders are very deliberate in their actions. They're not acting despite fear. They're acting on purpose. They're demonstrating courage every day, by trying, telling, and trusting.

Let's apply the principles in the last section to the leadership situation.

ONE THE COURAGE TO TRY.

The only constant in life is change! And with change comes big decisions. Big decisions have to be made, to improve, to update, to progress, and to move forward. And yes, your decisions and changes might be wrong. And you'll get a lesson or a blessing from the outcome.

But make the decision, implement the change and back yourself. Make it with the right information, with the right intent, and with the right foresight, and take your team forward.

LEADER ACTION

The old pros and cons strategy works every time (an oldie, but a goodie). Then, give yourself a timeframe in which to make the decision, and to try something new.

TWO THE COURAGE TO TRUST.

Leaders, please tune in. It's not quicker and better to do it yourself. Seriously, it's not. Trust people to do their jobs, with your support, as required—don't do it for them—and watch them shine. Trust is king if you want to develop a high performing team. Set expectations, set standards, and help your teams exceed them. And watch them transform during the process.

Catch yourself every time you know you're doing the work of your team. Hold yourself accountable for delegating, and for asking the right person to do the right work.

THREE THE COURAGE TO TELL.

There are so many things that you need to tell your team or team members. Whether it's about your vision, or about their performance. If you're saying it in your head (or to your leadership coach), it must be said aloud. Yes, my advice is always if you can tell me, you can tell them. Even if it might not be popular. Robust conversations need to be had. You owe it to the team or the person to have them. In a way that builds the relationship, not breaks it.

LEADER ACTION

Prepare, prepare, and prepare. Do a conversation planner, and make sure you know what you're going to say, and how, and why. Schedule it and communicate your message with care factor.

Yes, courageous leadership is about acting in spite of fear. But it's also about deliberate action. With an outcome in mind, and with a clear purpose.

Courage is a feeling piece. Once you have it, you can turn it into action—and into new ways of thinking. Have the courage now to think about how you think, and whether your coping style is affected by your courage—or your lack of it—when it comes time to deal with problems.

HOW TO ADOPT A PROBLEM—FOCUSED COPING STYLE TO DEAL WITH STRESS

We all cope with stressful situations differently, depending on the level and the nature of the stressful situation or event.

Over the past several decades researchers have identified the main coping styles of individuals, and it turns out that a problem-focused coping style is the best way to deal with stressors.

Stressors might include what psychologists call a 'stressful life event' (like moving house or losing a job), or it might include a major catastrophe at work (like a serious safety incident), or a flood, or an economic crisis.

As well as a problem-focused approach, there are two other coping styles identified in the research that we choose when coping with such events. These include emotional-focused and avoidant coping styles.

Here's an overview of each style.

ONE PROBLEM-FOCUSED COPING.

If you're someone who adopts a problem-focused approach to coping with stressors, you're someone gets into action. You're someone who addresses a problem head on, with a focus on taking action to address the issue or the challenge causing it.

Being problem focused is about taking ownership and responsibility for either solving or minimising the problem, with whatever resources are available to you at the time. This coping style is about doing a root-cause analysis and addressing what it is that's causing the stressor. And potentially having the additional focus to prevent reoccurrence.

Problem-focused coping is believed to be the most effective way to cope with stress, as it's action oriented. It means that the stressed person can take their focus off what they're feeling and focus on what they're doing, or on what others are doing. It's about collecting information, making decisions about the situation, and responding to the challenges of the situation with the clearest thinking possible.

TWO EMOTION-FOCUSED COPING.

The next best way to cope through a stressful life event is to take an emotion-focused approach. Emotion-focused coping is a type of stress management that attempts to reduce negative emotional responses associated with stress. Negative emotions such as embarrassment, fear, anxiety, depression, excitement, and frustration are reduced or removed by the individual by various methods of coping (Credit: Simply Psychology).

There are times when this coping strategy might be the most effective. Think about those times when the stressor is out of your control. Like an economic crash, or the death of a loved one. Or something else that can't be addressed through problem solving. This is actually the toughest coping strategy, as it takes a massive effort, and a commitment to emotional control. Things like mediation, breathing, focus change, or even medication are some of the tools you can use to adopt this coping strategy.

In saying that, this strategy is still a winner at any stage, and for me personally, the one that I go to. And most specifically, the tool that I pull out of the toolbox is the skill of reframing the situation. That is, putting a different spin on the stressor, and somehow, as hard as it can be, finding the positive. Turning the lesson (stressor) into a blessing (silver lining). Life gives us two types of emotional experiences—lessons or blessings. The sooner we can turn a lesson into a blessing, the quicker we can use emotional focus to help us get through stressful events.

THREE AVOIDANT-FOCUSED COPING.

As the name implies, an avoidant coping style in one where you pretend the event or the stressor doesn't exist, and you avoid dealing with it. Physically, and emotionally. This is easy for some people, but the vast majority of humans are not able to avoid a situation that causes them stress.

Generally, avoidance is only a short-term measure. At best. It does nothing to help you cope, really. In some cases, avoidance has been related to very negative outcomes for victims of cancer, say, where instead of addressing it, the victim avoided it. Pretended it didn't exist, and passed away.

For me, I feel like short-term avoidance could potentially lead to long-term issues. But I'd have to read some more research reports to validate that thought process.

When you're confronted by a stressor, get into action and do what you can to address the issue. Then, deal with the negative emotions that it causes, and try to reduce the impact of those negative emotions. Avoid the issue, as a last resort, remembering that you might eventually have to deal with it.

Be courageous in your coping style. There's a lot riding on your bravery— you need to be like Spiderman.

WHY BEING A LEADER IS LIKE BEING SPIDERMAN

Once upon a time there was a young man named Peter.

Peter had some tragedy in his life. He lost his parents, aged four, in a plane crash, and was raised by his Aunty May and Uncle Ben. More tragedy showed up in Peter's life, when he was bitten by a spider, and he was changed irreversibly. Then, a robber broke into their house, and Uncle Ben was fatally injured. Uncle Ben left a lasting legacy on Peter's life, when, in his dying moments, he shared with Peter the amazing wisdom that 'with great power, comes great responsibility.'

A great message, and a great story, about Peter Parker. Aka, Spiderman.

Peter (and anyone who watches the movies or follows the story) can learn from those words and remember them. Always. That's what leadership is about. Leaving a legacy that sets your team members up for success, with great advice. Not the opposite.

What does great responsibility mean, as a leader? It means to encourage transformation. It means to do no harm. It means to 'leave people better than you found them' (my personal mantra).

In our two-day leadership programs, we do an exercise where I ask the group if they can remember a time when a leader said something that was hurtful or harmful. And every hand goes up. 'Absolutely I can', is the response from the group members. 'Tell me more', I say...and the story generally starts like this: 'Well, it was twenty years ago, and I had a leader that was abusive/aggressive/abrupt...' 'And you still remember that?' I say. 'Of course, I'll never forget it', is the response. 'How could I? It was hurtful. And by the way', they say, 'that leader had no idea about how to treat humans...' 'Thanks for the story', I finish with, as I work my way around the room and close this little exercise about an hour later.

Then, we flip the script. 'So, team', I say. 'If a leader can have such an impact on you that you remember the stuff that they said twenty or more (often longer) years later, what might be the lesson?' The response is generally 'Don't be like that.' 'Great call', I say. 'Top job. Don't be the leader that's remembered for being crapola at human interaction' (or narcissistic, which is a common word I hear to describe poor leaders).

'Any other ideas?' I say then. Someone in the group will finally have an aha! moment and say (generally very excitedly): 'If leaders can have such a negative impact on people with what they say, why don't we focus on being a great leader, so that our legacy is one that people remember as being really positive, instead of the negative?' 'Absolutely, that's the key message', I affirm. Generally, just as excitedly!

Leadership, in my humble opinion, is the most important job on the planet after parenting (teachers are right up there, as are doctors and nurses and emergency services, of course). Leaders and teachers leave a lasting impact, one way or the other. To learn more from my favourite teacher, go to a recent newsletter here.

Back to leaders. With great power, comes great responsibility. But what does that really mean?

Here's a three-step process to keep that message front of mind.

ONE REMEMBER THAT YOUR TEAM IS WATCHING YOU.

As a leader, you're always on show. The age-old adage will apply in a hundred years just as it does now: what you walk past, you condone. And how you lead (and behave) will be reflected and be mirrored by your team. Yes, teams become a reflection of their leaders. Some leaders don't get this point. And the leader will say 'do as I say, not as I do', but your team watches more than they listen, which is human.

That's why leading by example is so important. And the most important thing is that your team are watching how you treat others. Are you firm, fair and friendly? Or are you playing favourites?

The time when you'll really need to be on your game is during a crisis event, or when you're under pressure. Pressure brings out worst in leaders, and they give themselves permission to default to react, rather than respond. Just ask Will Smith.

LEADER ACTION

With leadership comes the great responsibility to be the role model. Be how (the leader that you wish you had) was. Be the example of how to treat people the way they deserve to be treated. Be self-aware even when you're stressed out. Be aware of how you behave as a leader. Especially towards others.

TWO REMEMBER THAT YOUR TEAM IS LISTENING TO YOU.

As a leader, you'll face real challenges around leading and language. People hear what they want to hear. You think you say one thing, but they hear another. Do some research about confirmation bias and see what happens. And have an aha! moment about why our language connects with some of our team members and not others.

Most leaders don't realise the power of language. Just try using trigger words like no, disagree, wrong, but, and a range of others, and see what happens. Watch the reaction of your team member, as their amygdala fires and sends a message to their pituitary gland to release cortisol, which triggers the adrenal gland to release adrenaline so that the team member can be ready for a fight or to flight. Or to freeze or fawn. All in about .120 milliseconds. From just one word.

As important as step one is, just try making a commitment to a team member in an area that's important to them. Like their conditions, income, leave, or even their office space. They'll remember it until you follow through. So make sure you do. (See my sections on psychological safety.)

LEADER ACTION

With leadership comes the great responsibility to understand the language you use, and understand how to be less triggering as a leader, so you don't have a negative impact on your team members (sometimes, even without knowing it). Choose your words carefully, especially in high-pressure situations.

THREE DO NO HARM.

Be the leader who people remember for the right reasons. Not always popular decisions, but popular delivery of those same decisions.

This section is short, and the advice is simple: try not to be abusive, aggressive, or abrupt. These are the three major types of behaviour that hurt humans, and impact on their work.

Remember also that team members who aren't heard are hurt (which is why step two is important). When the team member says that they don't feel valued, it's code for 'just listen to me'. Follow step one and two, and you'll be on your way to doing no harm.

LEADER ACTION

With leadership comes the great responsibility to do no harm. Be clear on how you will and want to be remembered.

Focus on your leadership goals. Think about how you want to be remembered. If that goal and that commitment is always front of mind, you'll find the courage naturally as you work towards it.

Take some inspiration from wildly inspiring leaders—like William Wallace.

HOW TO LEAD LIKE WILLIAM WALLACE

Since the day I watched the movie *Braveheart*, I've never looked at leadership the same way. It was such a revelation, in its own way. You see, I probably don't watch movies like most people do, I watch them to learn something about the human species. And you sure can learn something from watching actors play the role of other humans.

If you haven't seen *Braveheart*, get on your favourite movie-streaming service and watch it. Don't thank me now. *Rotten Tomatoes* gave it a solid rating, and it won a string of awards. Yes, it was a little (extremely) factually incorrect if you know your Scottish history, but what it lacks in accuracy, it makes up for in action and excitement.

It's a love story, as much as it's a hero's journey. It's the story of William Wallace, who wasn't born into nobility, but who takes on the nobility, based on their poor leadership and the abuse of power. It's a story of a peasant who led a militia to take on the might of an invading nation, encouraging his own countrymen to stand and fight again oppression and tyranny.

What most people don't see, though, are the subtle leadership messages in the movie. Particularly in the key scenes. I firmly believe that movie makers are experts in the human psyche, and the producers of *Braveheart* (Mel Gibson's production company) nailed it. In this section, I'll unpack some of the hidden messages in some of the final scenes of the movie.

Let's look at leading like William Wallace—especially under pressure.

ONE LEADERSHIP IS TAKEN, NOT GIVEN.

William Wallace turned up and took control.

In one of the final scenes of the movie, the Scottish patriots (or the militia) were facing the might of the English army. Lochlan was leading the Scots, and he was trying to motivate the Scots to stay and fight. Against crazy odds. Totally outnumbered, and totally out-weaponed.

Lochlan thought he had situation covered. He was sitting atop his horse at the front of the Scottish army. And he was confident. Until William Wallace showed up. At that stage, no one knew that he was William Wallace. Not even Lochlan.

The difference was that William Wallace had a presence. William Wallace commanded respect. He told people who he was, but the Scots didn't believe him. He wasn't big enough to be William Wallace, who was apparently seven foot tall.

Once he started talking, though, the Scots listened. The pressure was on, the English were coming, and there wasn't a lot of time to motivate the Scots. But he did. And he thanked the Scots for presenting themselves on the battlefield. He was reverent, and at the same time totally committed. He was confident, and courageous. William Wallace didn't ask for permission to take charge, he just did.

Leadership is not about your job title. It's about your example, and your behaviour. Your team follow you because of who you are, not because of what your job role is.

TWO LEADERSHIP IS READING THE FIELD.

William Wallace called it as it was.

For me, this is the most important five seconds of the movie, and before I tell you what William Wallace said, let me give you the scenario. It's the very next part of the movie, after William Wallace arrives on the scene.

When Lochlan worked out it was William Wallace, he quickly shared with Wallace that the Scots were covered. They didn't need him. They told him that they had the whole situation in control. Which was interesting, because at the same time, some of the Scots were getting cold feet. They'd seen the English show up on the battlefield, and it was just a little too much for some of the Scots. They were scared. They needed to be motivated.

Ask anyone who's watched the film what the most important line in it was, and most will recite the famous line: 'They may take our lives, but they will never take our freedom!' But that isn't the most important line in the movie.

Fun fact: if you ever come to one of our leadership workshops, my favourite part (by far) is to unpack the great lines of the great business philosophers (aka, movie stars or famous humans). And when you know what the lines are from each of the famous people, you have to say it with passion. Imagine the room shouting out the freedom line from *Braveheart*. Or that unforgettable line from *Jerry McGuire*...you know the one.

If you were listening carefully to William Wallace, when Lochlan was telling Wallace that it was his army, and the Scots had it under control, Wallace said 'If this is your army, why does it go?' In other words, you're not motivating this army to stay and fight. For me, this is the best line in the movie. And leaders everywhere: if this is your team, why are they leaving?

Leadership is about being honest about the situation you're in. It's not about beating around the bush. Especially when you're under pressure, you need to be direct, and make your words count.

THREE LEADERSHIP IS NEVER GIVING UP.

William Wallace stayed committed, even on his death bed.

For me, the final scene in the movie sums up the life of a leader. To the very end of his life, William Wallace was committed to one thing. Freedom. Even when he was being tortured by the English, and his torturers wanted to hear him say one word—*mercy*.

It wasn't Wallace who said that word, though, it was the crowd. Pleading for mercy and pleading for an end to the torture. The crowd was mainly English, so it was amazing to see the impact that Wallace had on not only his own team, but also on the English.

How truthful it is, who knows. He wouldn't have been able to scream out, but he did. Instead of muttering the word *mercy*, he screamed at the top of his voice, *freedom*. That one word that had driven his life's purpose, and his life's work. He died for freedom. Like in the movie, Wallace is said to have accepted his execution without any resistance. And with a brave heart. He even made a final confession to a priest and read from the book of Psalms before his torture and execution.

Leadership under pressure is about staying committed until the situation has passed or the work is done. For some leaders, this is never. For some leaders, building their business, their team, or the organisation is their life's work. And it's work that they'll never stop doing.

Lead like William Wallace. Remember that leadership is taken, not given. Read the field, and never give up. And be courageous—especially when it's decision-making time, and people are looking to you.

I'D HAVE LESS WORK IF LEADERS DID THIS ONE THING

The more senior the leader, the bigger the decisions they have to make. But some senior leaders don't make the decisions that they need to. They put decisions off. They postpone decision making. They let decisions linger. And it doesn't help their teams.

I understand it. And I can empathise with putting off decision making. Sometimes you need more information. Sometimes you need more input. Sometimes you need more ideas.

I was sitting having a lunch chat recently with a leader, who was explaining their frustration with their leader. Their leader was sitting on some key decisions that my lunch partner was waiting on, and the person I was speaking to was beside themselves with anxiety and other negative emotions. They just weren't able to do their job properly, waiting on their leader to make key decisions. Like decisions around people, processes, or major purchases. They're the big ones.

Following our lunch chat, I went back through my coaching notes, and at least three out of four sessions discussed decisions that needed to be made by the leader of the person that I'm coaching. For most of the people I coach (well over 700), needing their leader to make a decision is a big issue.

So what stops leaders making decisions, and how can they get into decision-making mode?

ONE LACK OF CLARITY.

When the goal of a decision isn't clear, it can be hard to make the right choice. A leader may struggle to make a decision if they don't understand the desired outcome, or are missing the parts that make up an informed decision. The goal and outcomes of every decision need to be very clear.

LEADER ACTION

Get the information, input, and ideas you need. Make a commitment to your team, that you'll make the decision after getting all of the information you need. Set a decision deadline.

TWO FEAR OF FAILURE.

Fear of failure can be a major obstacle to decision making, especially when it comes to important decisions. Leaders may be concerned that their decision could have negative consequences, or that they may make the wrong choice. This fear can be crippling enough to stop them from making a decision that needs to be made.

LEADER ACTION

Fear of failure stems from worrying about what could go wrong as a result of the decision. The trick is to reframe your thinking to work through what could go right, instead.

THREE PERSONAL BIASES.

A leader's personal beliefs and preferences can also influence their decision making. They may be more likely to make a decision that aligns with their values, even if it's not the best course of action. We lean on our values when we need to make any big decisions, so it's important to be clear on what your personal values are, and how they align with the values of the business—otherwise, you'll be prone to bias.

LEADER ACTION

Make sure you know your business's values, and your own. Knowing where you differ from your business will help you have a clearer picture of where your biases are.

Leaders need to be aware of factors that can stop them from making decisions, and they should strive to be courageous in doing it, even when it's difficult.

Take the time to gather all the information you need to make an informed decision, and be courageous enough to consider your own biases. With practice and dedication, you can overcome the obstacles to decision making, and become an effective—and courageous—decision maker.

ACTIVITY 2.5
BE COURAGEOUS

Answering the following questions will encourage you to think about what you can do to lead more courageously, in the process of upskilling your leadership. Thinking about how to be more courageous in leading your team through difficult times, and developing a stronger problem-focused coping style, can help you improve your communication and grow your confidence to get the best results from your team.

Do you have the courage to try, even though you could fail?

Can you trust your team enough to hand off important tasks? Why, or why not?

Do you use problem-, emotion-, or avoidant-focused coping? How is it working out for you?

Do you think your team members are learning effective strategies by watching and listening to you? Why, or why not?

Answer honestly. Do you think your team members follow your instructions because of your role, or because of your character and example?

Answer honestly. What personal biases are influencing your decision making?

AFTERWORD

If you're still with me, congratulations on making it this far. And thanks for finding me engaging enough that you decided not to put this book down and never look at it again.

What I hope has kept you connected to my words is the resilience with which I wrote them. I hope you can see how creating conscious control helps you to develop as a leader, to overcome the urge to lose it under pressure—no matter what's happening in that moment—and to lead your teams with emotional consistency and care factor.

I was not always a good leader. But now, I hope, I'm a leader that people will remember for the right reasons. I hope you can see how learning to respond, and not react, can help you become a better human. And that being courageous can help you to trust others enough to connect in meaningful ways, and to lead your team every day with integrity.

This book isn't the answer to all of your leadership woes. But it's the beginning of the process. A process that needs to start from within, by understanding your own triggers, fears, and coping methods, so you can put away what doesn't work, and put on what does.

If you're an old-school leader, the one that I wrote this book for, congratulations on getting through a book you probably weren't very comfortable reading. See how learning emotional literacy makes you more professional, not less? And how investing in care factor makes for a more productive team, and not a workplace in emotional chaos?

If you're a new-age leader, the one that I wrote this book for, congratulations on getting through a book you probably thought was going to be a lot less work. See how empathy, not sympathy, helps you support your team members through BOOM events without burning you out? Your consistency, conscious control, and courage are allowing your team and organisation to benefit from your growth and upgraded skills.

There's a lot more to learn about people, and yourself. Go and get stuck into whatever piques your interest: developing emotional literacy; how to manage your amygdala hijack; how to be a stoic leader. This book is the beginning, and as long as you're leading, there shouldn't be an end.

Learn more from me. I have a bunch of books and a team of people who can help you become a better leader. Or don't learn more from me. Learn from anyone whose leadership is inspiring to you in any way. Or anyone whose leadership has caused you stress, or duress, or to decide to never, ever lead your team like they led you. Go learn how to lead with care factor, and courage, and enough insight to know that leading by example is the most powerful way to guide your team towards professional development.

If you don't remember anything I've taught you in this book, remember how it made you feel. If it filled you with hope and optimism, and overwhelmed you with the urge to commit to being a better leader, good. Go do it. If it filled you with dread and shame about how bad your leadership really is, good. Go get better at it.

Either way, you got this far because you're becoming reflective. You're learning how to think differently. You're learning how to react differently. You're learning how to answer the big questions—including why you're a leader, and why you do what you do.

Congratulations on finishing this book. You're upskilling your leadership. Keep going. Every learning is getting you closer to where you want to be.

REFERENCES

1. Alexander, F. M. (1924). *Constructive Conscious Control of the Individual*. The Irdeat complete edition. Mouritz.

2. Algoe, S. B. (2012). Find, Remind, and Bind: The Functions of Gratitude in Everyday Relationships. Social and Personality Psychology Compass, 6(6), 455-469.

3. Bingham, J. (1999). *The Courage to Start: A Guide to Running for Your Life*. Touchstone.

4. Bowman, J. (2020). *Stoicism, Enkrasia and Happiness: How Stoic Philosophy Can Bring Happiness*. Independently published.

5. Alexander, F. M. (1924). Constructive Conscious Control of the Individual. The Irdeat complete edition. Mouritz.

6. Burns, J. M. (1978). *Leadership*. New York, NY: Harper & Row Publishers.

7. Chamorro-Premuzic, T. (2018). *5 Ways Leaders Accidentally Stress Out Their Employees*. Harvard Business Review. Retrieved from https://hbr.org/2020/05/5-ways-leaders-accidentally-stress-out-their-employees

8. Chopra, D. (2010). *The Soul of Leadership: Unlocking Your Potential for Greatness*. Harmony Books.

9. Covey, S. M. R. (2006). *The Speed of Trust: The One Thing That Changes Everything*. Free Press.

10. Fitzgerald, M. (2011). *Iron War: Dave Scott, Mark Allen, & the Greatest Race Ever Run*. VeloPress.

11. Goleman, D. (1995). *Emotional Intelligence: Why It Can Matter More Than IQ*. New York, NY: Bantam Books.

12. Kahneman, D. (2011). *Thinking, Fast and Slow*. Farrar, Straus and Giroux.

13. Lassiter, C. W. (2015). *Everyday Courage School Leaders: Taking Action in the Face of Risk*. Teachers College Press.

14. Mackey, J., Mcintosh, S., & Phipps, C. (2020). *Conscious Leadership: Elevating Humanity Through Business*. Harvard Business Review Press.

15. Marsh, C. (2003). A psycho-physiological comparison of post-traumatic and prolonged duress stress disorders. *Behavioural and Cognitive Psychotherapy, 31*(1), 109-112.

16. Mirvis, P. H., & Googins, B. K. (2010). Stages of Corporate Citizenship: An Integrated Framework for the Study of Corporate Social Responsibility. In W. Visser, D. Matten, M. Pohl, & N. Tolhurst (Eds.), *The Oxford Handbook of Corporate Social Responsibility* (pp. 67-83). Oxford University Press.

17. Nelson-Isaacs, S. (2019). *Living in Flow: The Science of Synchronicity and How Your Choices Shape Your World*. North Atlantic Books.

18. Paulhus, D. L., & Williams, K. M. (2002). The dark triad of personality: narcissism, machiavellianism, and psychopathy. *Journal of research in personality, 36*(6), 556-563.

19. Pury, C. L. S., & Lopez, S. J. (2016). The psychology of courage: Modern research on an ancient virtue. *American Psychological Association*.

20. Robbins, T. *Discover the 6 Human Needs.* Retrieved from https://www.tonyrobbins.com/mind-meaning/do-you-need-to-feel-significant/

21. Rossouw, P. J. (2020). The Predictive 6-Factor Resilience Scale: Neurobiological Fundamentals and Organizational Application. *Journal of Business and Psychology, 35*(4), 499-511.

22. Safe Work Australia. (2018). *Work-related psychological health and safety: A systematic approach to meeting your duties*. Safe Work Australia. Retrieved from https://www.safeworkaustralia.gov.au/doc/work-related-psychological-health-and-safety-systematic-approach-meeting-your-duties-archived

23. Safe Work Australia. (2011). *Guide to Preventing and Responding to Workplace Bullying*. Retrieved from https://www.safeworkaustralia.gov.au/doc/guide-preventing-and-responding-workplace-bullying

24. Scott, K. (2017). *Radical Candor: Be a Kick-Ass Boss Without Losing Your Humanity*. St. Martin's Press.

25. Scott, S. (2002). *Fierce Conversations: Achieving Success at Work and in Life, One Conversation at a Time*. Berkley.

26. Sheldon, K. M., & Lyubomirsky, S. (2006). How to increase and sustain positive emotion: The effects of expressing gratitude and visualizing best possible selves. *The Journal of Positive Psychology, 1*(2), 73–82.

27. Singh, P. (2016). Influence of Leaders Intrapersonal Competencies on Employee Job Satisfaction. *Global Business and Management Research, 8*(2), 57-65.

GLOSSARY

Akratic. Characterised by a weakness of will, resulting in action against one's better judgement.

Allocation. A consultative process of assigning tasks and responsibilities involving engagement, discussion and agreement between leaders and their team members (as opposed to delegation).

Amygdala hijack. Coined by psychologist Daniel Goleman. Where processing emotions such as fear, anger, and anxiety, overrides the prefrontal cortex, the part of the brain responsible for reasoning and decision making.

Avoidant-focused coping. A style of coping where the person pretends the event or stressor doesn't exist and avoids dealing with it.

Bandwidth (leadership and management). The capacity or limit of an individual or team to effectively lead and manage a certain number of people, projects, or responsibilities.

Big 3 leadership mandates. The obligations of leaders to the organisation, to the team, and to the self. Also known as values, transformation, and control (VTC).

BOOM Event. An unexpected serious or catastrophic event in the workplace or the lives of an organisation's employees.

Bystander effect. Psychological phenomenon where the inhibiting influence of the presence of others affects a person's willingness to help someone in need.

Care factor. Strategy for effective leadership involving giving team members time, using conversation techniques around psychological safety, psychological empowerment, and psychological connection, and being courageous in the process.

CBT. Cognitive Behavioural Therapy. A form of psychological treatment or therapy that focuses on changing negative or unhelpful thoughts and behaviours in order to improve mental health and wellbeing.

Challenger safety. One of the four stages of psychological safety in teams in Timothy R Clark's theory on how safe team members feel to speak up, and offer ideas, opinions, and views without the fear of resentment, ridicule, or rejection.

Conscious control. The ability to intentionally and actively regulate one's thoughts, emotions, and behaviours using conscious awareness and decision-making processes. Includes emotional, behavioural, and situational control.

Conscious leadership. A leadership approach that emphasises self-awareness, personal growth, and the cultivation of positive relationships and organisational culture. Conscious leaders are aware of their own thoughts, feelings, and behaviours, and how they affect others, and create a supportive, inclusive, and purpose-driven workplace.

C-Suite team. The group of top executives in an organisation (usually including the CEO, COO, CFO, CMO, CTO, and CHRO) who are responsible for setting the strategic direction of the organisation, making major decisions, and overseeing the day-to-day operations of the business to achieve its goals and objectives.

Dark Triad. A psychological term to describe three personality traits that are characterised by a lack of empathy, a tendency toward exploitative behaviour, and a focus on self-interest and personal gain. Comprised of three traits including narcissism, machiavellianism, and psychopathy. Associated with negative outcomes in personal and professional relationships, and in mental health and wellbeing.

Delegation. A process of assigning tasks and responsibilities to team members without collaboration with or input from their leader.

Deficit dialogue dilemma. A term to describe the challenge of effectively communicating and building understanding across different perspectives and worldviews in an organisation. Arises when individuals or groups with differing viewpoints are unable or unwilling to engage in productive dialogue with one another due to factors such as ideological polarisation, social or cultural barriers, or a lack of trust or respect between groups, leading to a breakdown in communication, a lack of cooperation and collaboration, and organisational dysfunction.

DiSC profile. A personality assessment tool designed to help individuals understand their behavioural preferences and communication styles. The DiSC model categorises people into four primary behavioural styles: Dominance (direct and assertive communication style and focus on results), Influence (persuasive and enthusiastic communication style and focus on building relationships), Steadiness (patient and supportive communication style focused on collaboration), and Conscientiousness (a cautious communication style and focus on quality and accuracy).

Disciplined courage. The courage you need to stand up for your position and maintain your commitments when things are going badly.

Duress. Wrongful or unlawful coercion applied by another person (usually a leader). Distinct from normal stress, strain or pressure.

EI (also EQ). Theory of emotional intelligence heavily influenced by Daniel Goleman. Applied in profiling tools to assess social management on measures of empathy, sensitivity, and appreciation; service, compassion, and benevolence; holistic communication; situational perceptual awareness; and interpersonal development.

Emotion-focused coping. A type of stress management that attempts to reduce negative emotional responses associated with stress. Negative emotions such as embarrassment, fear, anxiety, depression, excitement, and frustration are reduced or removed by various coping methods.

Empathetic courage. The courage to challenge your personal biases so you're better placed to experience what others are going through and to understand why.

Empathy. The key skill for leading under pressure. A process beginning with cognitive understanding of what someone is going though, and ending with doing something (where possible) to support them.

Golden Rule (of communication). Treating others how you would want to be treated.

Groupthink. A phenomenon that occurs when a group of individuals reaches a consensus without critical reasoning or evaluation of the consequences or alternatives.

Growth Mindset. A concept popularised by psychologist Carol Dweck. A belief that individuals can develop their abilities and intelligence through hard work, dedication, and perseverance, and that talents and abilities are not fixed, but can be improved through effort and learning.

High Reliability Organisation (HRO). An organisation that operates in complex, high-risk environments where the consequences of errors can be severe (e.g. nuclear power plants, air traffic control centres, and hospitals). Characterised by a strong safety culture, a commitment to continuous improvement, and a focus on identifying and managing risks.

Intellectual courage. The courage you need to turn your knowledge into action in the workplace.

Lencioni Model. A popular leadership development and team-building framework developed by author and consultant Patrick Lencioni. Provides a clear and actionable roadmap for building effective teams, involving trust, productive conflict, commitment, accountability, and a focus on achieving outcomes and results through both individual effort and collaboration.

LMX (Leader-Member Exchange). A leadership theory that focuses on the relationship between a leader and their individual followers or team members. Suggests that the quality of the relationship between a leader and their team members can have a significant impact on individual and team performance.

Manipulative Insincerity. Insincerity in your responses, feedback or praises, without the sugar-coating, that's delivered with the intent to hurt or harm.

Metacognition. Described as 'thinking about thinking'. How you learn and gain knowledge, and then how you apply that knowledge.

Normal Accident Theory. A theory the field of system safety engineering that explains why complex technological systems are susceptible to catastrophic failures or accidents. Suggests that accidents are an inevitable result of the complexity and interconnectedness of modern technological systems, and that no amount of planning, engineering, or design can completely eliminate the possibility of an accident occurring.

Obnoxious Aggression. Being clear, but not kind (also known as 'brutal honesty'), and unlike manipulative insincerity. Unintentionally causes hurt through poor delivery of the message.

Platinum rule (of communication). Communicating with others in the communication style they prefer, not the style you prefer.

PR6. The six elements of resilience developed by Jurie Rossouw. Includes vision, collaboration, composure, health, tenacity, and reasoning.

Problem-focused coping. Addressing the root cause of a stressor, and taking ownership and responsibility for either solving or minimising the problem with whatever resources are available at the time.

Project Aristotle. A research project initiated by Google in 2012 to study what makes a successful team. Identifies key factors that contribute to high-performing teams and improve team effectiveness and productivity, including psychological safety, dependability, structure and clarity, meaning, and impact.

Psychological safety. A concept describing the extent to which team members feel that they are respected, valued, and that their contributions are important, and how safe and comfortable they feel expressing their thoughts, ideas, and concerns without fear of negative consequences. Encourages open communication, promotes learning and innovation, and can improve team performance.

RACI matrix. A project management tool used to define and clarify roles and responsibilities within a team. RACI stands for Responsible, Accountable, Consulted, and Informed. The matrix is used to assign these roles to team members for each task or activity in a project.

Radical candour. A leadership approach that allows and encourages team members to share ideas and information, and contributes to the psychological safety of the workplace.

Ruinous Empathy. Insincerity in responses, feedback, or praises, and sugar-coating of criticism, to avoid the other person feeling bad.

Siloing. When leaders or team members don't operate as part of a team, but focus on their work, department, or business unit without regard for the rest of the organisation.

Senior leadership team (SLT). Also called Senior leadership group. A team of leaders of different levels that manage the running of the business to help it reach its goals.

Sunset-first approach. Letting the 'sun set' on a major decision or the execution of a major decision, i.e., thinking and 'sleeping on it' before coming back the next day to make a decision.

Systems Leadership. The practice of leading and managing complex systems, such as organisations, by focusing on the interrelationships and interconnectedness of the various components and stakeholders involved. Seeks to engage all members of the system in collaborative problem solving, decision making, and innovation. Requires a range of skills, including communication, collaboration, systems thinking, data analysis, and strategic planning.

Team Charter. A document that outlines the purpose, goals, roles, and expectations of a team so all members have a clear understanding of the team's mission, objectives, and expectations for performance.

Team management systems (TMS). A set of tools and assessments used for profiling and managing teams. Provides a framework for understanding team dynamics and individual preferences, and helps team leaders to identify and leverage the strengths of their team members.

Tell courage. The courage to articulate goals and objectives to the team.

Tepid leadership. A laissez-faire, 'hands-off' approach to leadership where the leader doesn't sufficiently support the team members.

Toxic Workplace Culture. An environment in which employees experience persistent negative attitudes, behaviours, and practices that have a harmful impact on their wellbeing and job performance. Common characteristics include lack of trust, bullying and harassment, poor communication, high levels of stress, lack of recognition and reward, low morale, and resistance to change.

Transactional leadership. A contingent reward-based style of leadership where the leader expects strict compliance with business practice.

Transformational leadership. A process in which leaders and followers help each other to advance to a higher level of morale and motivation.

Trust courage. The courage to trust team members to reach a goal themselves.

Trust-less leadership. Aka micromanagement, where the leader does not allow team members sufficient responsibility and room for professional growth.

Tuckman Model. A widely recognised model in the field of team dynamics developed by psychologist Bruce Tuckman in 1965. Identifies four stages of group development: forming, storming, norming, and performing.

Try Courage. The courage to try and reach a goal despite the risk of failure.

Values, Transformation, and Control (VTC). A theoretical framework developed by Cameron and Quinn in the 1980s to understand organisational change and development. Posits that culture is made up of three main components: values, transformation, and control. Based on these components, organisations can be classified into one of four categories (clan, adhocracy, market, and hierarchy cultures).

360-degree survey feedback. A type of performance appraisal tool that provides an individual with feedback from multiple sources. Feedback is gathered from various sources, including the individual's manager, peers, direct reports, and customers or stakeholders.

5P process for facilitating workshops. Involves purpose (clearly define and share), process (how to run it and what resources are needed), people (who needs to be there), performance (facilitating questions, encouraging conversation, listening and documenting discussion), and polish (close out process to add value to the time the team has committed to the process).

7 states and traits. Skills for effective leadership that include learning, engaging, articulating, demonstration, empathy, resilience, and safety.

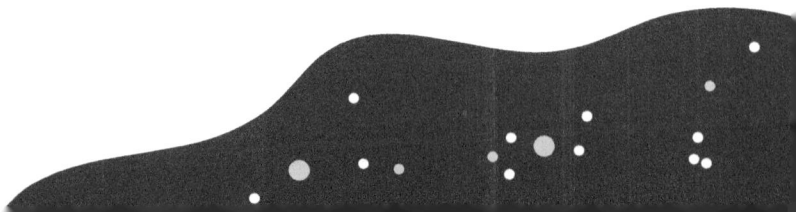

OTHER BOOKS
IN THIS SERIES

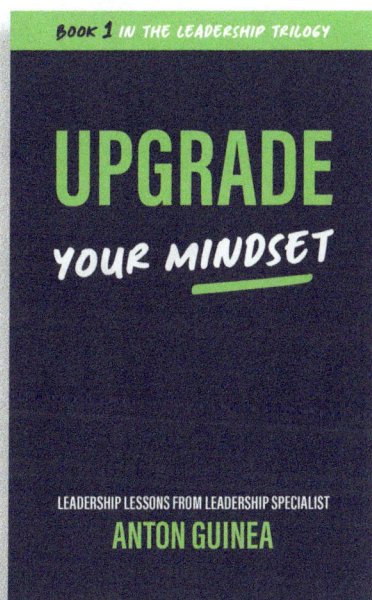

BOOK *1* IN THE LEADERSHIP TRILOGY

UPGRADE
YOUR MINDSET

LEADERSHIP LESSONS FROM LEADERSHIP SPECIALIST
ANTON GUINEA

BOOK *3* IN THE LEADERSHIP TRILOGY

UPLIFT
YOUR TEAMS

LEADERSHIP LESSONS FROM LEADERSHIP SPECIALIST
ANTON GUINEA

Learn how to introspect, put things in perspective, and cope better under pressure as a leader by upgrading your mindset.

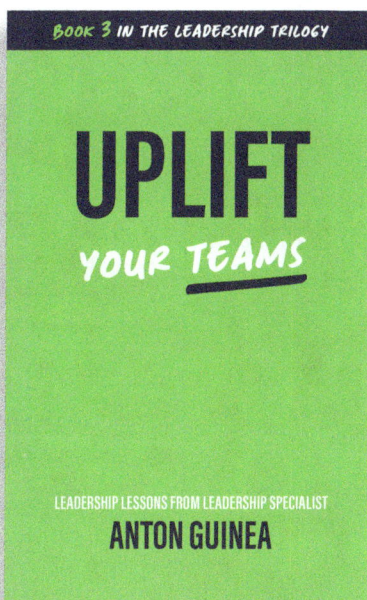

Learn the fine art of facilitation, how to deal with a team in turmoil, and how to use a radical candour approach to uplift your teams.

ABOUT *ANTON*

Anton's life and work experiences have led him to become a visionary thought leader, delivering the right mix of empathy and enthusiasm in all his programs. His energy, engagement, and enterprise thinking is helping leaders develop into transformational and inspiring role models, who uplift the people in their care, and create high-performing teams.

Anton is a widely regarded keynote speaker. But he is also a qualified Resilience Coach, and a graduate of psychology and human resources. He's supported by The Guinea Group team of professionals, who share his commitment to service and over-delivering for leaders and organisations within Australia and across the world.

This valuable experience, paired with his unshakeable commitment to his 'why'—leaving people better than he found them—underpins his truly transformative programs.

LOOKING FOR A
WORLD-CLASS SPEAKER
FOR YOUR NEXT LIVE OR VIRTUAL LEADERSHIP EVENT?

A professional speaker since 2005, Anton has worked with global organisations within Australia and across the world.

With a noteworthy ability to help people to think differently, Anton's speaking packages also comprise pre- and post-event support and resources, helping leaders and their teams to maintain their commitment to growth and development in the lifelong process of upgrading their mindsets.

Anton is a skilled keynote speaker. But he's also a researcher, and a former tradesperson experienced in working under pressure and for poor-performing leaders. This valuable experience, paired with his unshakeable commitment to his 'why'—leaving people better than he found them—underpins his truly transformative performance as a speaker.

To find out more about how Anton can help you to find your purpose, and to build a meaningful and rewarding career, visit us here.

www.ingramcontent.com/pod-product-compliance
Lightning Source LLC
Chambersburg PA
CBHW072149020426

42334CB00018B/1928